Crossing Languages and Research Methods

Analyses of Adult Foreign Language Reading

A volume in
Research in Second Language Learning
JoAnn Hammadou Sullivan, *Series Editor*

Crossing Languages and Research Methods

Analyses of Adult Foreign Language Reading

Edited by

Cindy Brantmeier
Washington University in St. Louis

INFORMATION AGE PUBLISHING, INC.
Charlotte, NC • www.infoagepub.com

Library of Congress Cataloging-in-Publication Data

Crossing languages and research methods analyses of adult foreign language reading / edited by Cindy Brantmeier.
    p. cm. – (Research in second language learning)
  Includes bibliographical references.
  ISBN 978-1-60752-285-0 (pbk.) – ISBN 978-1-60752-286-7 (hardcover) – ISBN 978-1-60752-287-4 (e-book)
1. Language and languages–Study and teaching. 2. Second language acquisition. 3. Multicultural education. I. Brantmeier, Cindy.
  P53.755.C76 2009
  418.0071–dc22

                                    2009035543

Printed in the United States of America

I dedicate this book to my children, Anjali and Gavin Brantmeier Prabhakar.
One of the best gifts I can give you is that of multilingualism.

CONTENTS

FOREWORD

In 2002, this series was launched with its first volume, *Literacy and the Second Language Learner*, which contained many noteworthy research studies in the learning and teaching of second language reading. The selection of this theme for the series' entry on the scene is one demonstration of the importance of the topic of second language reading. Because reading plays a key role in the act of acquiring new knowledge, it is important to understand this complex process. The series again explores this multifaceted and fruitful area of inquiry in this, its seventh volume. In recent years, an explosion of work that strives to create a more complete understanding of second language reading has occurred and researchers today are making gains in fitting together a model of second language reading (Bernhardt, 2005). Yet, as Roger Brown wrote in 1996 about language learning in general, we still find the following applicable to second language reading research:

> Psychologists find it exciting when a complex mental phenomenon—something intelligent and slippery—seems about to be captured by a mechanical model. We yearn to see the model succeed. But when, at the last minute, the phenomenon proves too much for the model and darts off on some uncapturable tangent, there is something in us that rejoices at the defeat. (Quoted in Brown, 2007, p. 4)

Although we may "rejoice," as Brown wryly puts it, at the complexity of what we study, we also risk the ire that has plagued researchers in first language reading. Historically, much contentious debate and unrealistic expectations have marred inquiry into first language reading processes instruction (Kim, 2008) and the public at large has suffered from what the

Crossing Languages and Research Methods, pages ix–x
Copyright © 2009 by Information Age Publishing
All rights of reproduction in any form reserved.

educational historian Harvey J. Graff (1994) calls the "historical myth" that "literacy, learning, schooling, and education are simple, unproblematic notions…" (p. 44). For second language educators, that myth translates into the complaint that "I studied French, Spanish, or [name your language], for two years and I didn't learn a thing." Such a complaint is usually leveled at the language instructors. And as foreign language programs struggle to survive, research into better understanding of the processes of second language learning is of urgent, critical importance. Educators' ability to assist second language readers to gain meaning independently from a variety of sources is still not at a level that all would consider satisfactory. As part of that elusive hunt for a fuller understanding, this current volume brings together a range of high quality analyses of adult foreign language reading. It provides important research findings that will assist foreign language readers and those who support their efforts.

REFERENCES

Bernhardt, E. (2005). Progress and procrastination in second language reading. *Annual Review of Applied Linguistics, 25,* 133–150.

Brown, H. D. (2007). *Principles of language learning and teaching* (5th ed.). White Plains, NY: Pearson Education.

Graff, H. J. (1994). Literacy, myths and legacies: Lessons from the history of literacy. In L. T. Verhoeven (Ed.), *Studies in written language and literacy: Vol. 1, Functional literacy: Theoretical issues and educations implications* (pp. 37–60). Amsterdam: John Benjamins.

Kim, J. S. (2008). Research and the reading wars. *Phi Delta Kappan, 89*(5), 372–375.

CHAPTER 1

INTRODUCTION

Foreign Language Reading Research with Adults: A Selected Survey of Variables and Methodologies

Cindy Brantmeier

This book consists of a collection of chapters that reflect the complex nature of foreign language reading with adults. Each report offers new empirical evidence to substantiate comprehensive theories of foreign language reading. This volume is not an exhaustive representation of all variables involved in reading research and theory; rather, it serves to advance existing knowledge on the topic. The research presented involves a variety of languages, different stages of L2 acquisition, and diverse research methodologies. Each paper went through a rigorous review process and was anonymously reviewed by applied linguists in the field. The purpose of bringing these papers together is to illustrate the diversity and unique perspectives of each researcher while simultaneously showing that there are pieces of a shared, comprehensive, and interactive theory reflected in each paper. The book is primarily intended for those concerned with data driven evi-

Crossing Languages and Research Methods, pages 1–6
Copyright © 2009 by Information Age Publishing
All rights of reproduction in any form reserved.

dence to support second language reading research, theory and practice with adults.

A COMPREHENSIVE, INTERACTIVE THEORY

In a synthesis of up-to-date work on first-language (L1) reading conducted by cognitive psychologists, Rayner and Pollatsek (1989) comment on how models and theories are not always comprehensive and consequently may be exasperating. They borrow Carr's (1982) definition of *theory* and *model* and adapt it to the reading process (p. 25). Carr (1982) defines theory as a set of principles (assumptions or rules) that together constitutes a verbal description of an interesting phenomenon and an explanation of how or why the phenomenon happens. A theory also defines the important characteristics of the phenomenon that are then included in a model. A model offers a description of the major working parts of a real-life process (such as second-language reading). The description captures the most important characteristics of each part's operation, though it may leave out large amounts of detail.

There are a number of models of the L2 reading process, but most comprehensive, interactive one that first captured bottom-up and top-down processing is the Bernhardt Model (1991). The Bernhardt Model combines both cognitive and social perspectives on reading as it offers both text-driven and reader-based views of the L2 reading process, and it does not ignore the fact that L2 readers approach a text from their first-language framework. This integrative perspective assumes that both reading development and reading proficiency exist. The model encompasses micro-level features, such as word recognition, phonemic/graphemic features, and syntax, as well as macro-level features, such as background knowledge and perceptions (both knowledge-driven features), that are plotted against each other according to the axes. Word recognition is defined as the attachment of semantic value, and phonemic/graphemic decoding entails the process involved in how L2 readers are influenced by the way words look or sound when interpreting a text. Syntactic feature recognition involves the interpretation of the relationship of words (Bernhardt, 1991). To borrow Bernhardt's explanation of a micro-level feature of the model, "...word recognition, represented as an exponential curve, posits that in the early stages of proficiency errors that can be attributed to vocabulary difficulties are fairly common" (p. 170). Background knowledge and perception is the reconciliation of each part of the text to preceding and succeeding elements. To clarify a macro-level aspect, Bernhardt (1991) states that with background knowledge "... the rate of errors due to both content knowledge and knowledge constructed during comprehension decreases as proficiency increases" (p. 170). Bernhardt also addresses the issue of metacognition, or the extent to which the reader is thinking about what is being read. In order to test and validate this model, studies have been conducted on all aspects of the theory.

Most recently, Bernhardt (2000, 2003) offers a conceptualization of L2 reading that captures reading over time (see Bernhardt, 2000, p. 103). This most recent model emphasizes the development and progress of the reader, and it also leaves room for the unexplained variance in L2 reading. The book attempts to validate a comprehensive, interactive theory of L2 reading by researching both micro- and macro-level features of the reading process with adult learners of several different languages at different levels of language instruction and with diverse research methodologies.

McMillion and Shaw examine comprehension and compensatory processing of readings from textbooks with very advanced Swedish learners of English and L1 readers of English. They specifically examine speed and efficiency measures and comprehension across different assessment tasks. Lee and Binkowski investigate the comprehension of Spanish future-tense morphology while reading in an L2. They examine the effects of pre-reading questions, input frequency, and lexical temporal indicators on reading comprehension. With students enrolled in German courses, Schueller explores the effects of strategic training on male and female reading comprehension. More specifically, she analyzes the effect of pre-reading strategy training on conceptually driven top-down strategies and text-bound bottom-up strategies. With advanced learners of Spanish, Brantmeier and Dragiyski utilize a metacognitive strategy inventory with different text types and various comprehension assessment tasks to examine associations for global reading strategies, problem solving strategies, and support strategies with comprehension. Farley and Keating investigate whether low-level learners of Spanish can perform as well as or better than more advanced bilinguals on a word-level reading categorization task. The authors examine whether the learners used concept mediation on tasks, and they also account for reaction times. Maxim utilizes classroom observations, learner interviews, and analyses of learner writing to characterize how six advanced FL learners of German viewed and responded to an explicit instructional approach to narrow reading and writing development. Young and Nacuma investigate what happens when misunderstandings occur while reading in a second language. They analyze written recalls of a Spanish passage that contain a higher number of misunderstandings compared to other passages with low numbers of misunderstandings in the recalls.

L2 READING RESEARCH METHODS

The authors in the present volume employ multiple research methodologies to illuminate the various aspects involved in the complex reading process. Some researchers emphasize what the reader does *while* reading—the process. Other investigators concentrate on what gets comprehended or stored in memory *after* reading—the product. This volume highlights both the process and the product of reading, with quantitative as well as qualitative research methodologies and procedures. In both quantitative and qualitative investigations concerning second-language reading comprehension, justification for instrumentation is motivated and validated by a thorough review of related research. The following discussion serves as a brief overview of the research methods used by L2 reading researchers.

QUANTITATIVE INQUIRY IN L2 READING

Quantitative inquiry seeks to explain L2 reading primarily through objective measurement and quantitative analysis. The quantitative researcher is detached from the phenomenon, and heavy emphasis is placed on the procedures that must be followed faithfully. Figure 1.1 presents a schematic review of research components for inquiries about L2 reading comprehension. The arrows designate the typical sequence in which the mechanisms are executed in the research process.

The first step is the development of a research problem. The research problem is a general issue about L2 reading that involves an area of concern to researchers and/or instructors. Next, the researcher reviews previous investigations related to the factors involved in the research problem (Bernhardt, 1991). The following step entails defining the research problem as specifically as possible while keeping in mind that the questions should be feasible, clear, significant, and ethical (Fraenkel & Wallen, 1996). Most L2 reading researchers utilize participants enrolled in second-language programs at a university or a private language institute because it is extremely difficult to select a random sample population to study. Researchers find a previously existing instrument or develop a new instrument that is grounded in previous research, and those instruments are often piloted several times with participants to ensure reliability and objectivity. Quantitative researchers include a detailed description of instruments created and used to collect data from the participants as well as a rationale for their use. Next, the researcher determines the procedures to be executed in the study. These methods are described in detail so that the experiment can be replicated after publication. The next stage, data analysis, includes both the scoring procedures utilized for the assessment tasks as well as the statistical techniques,

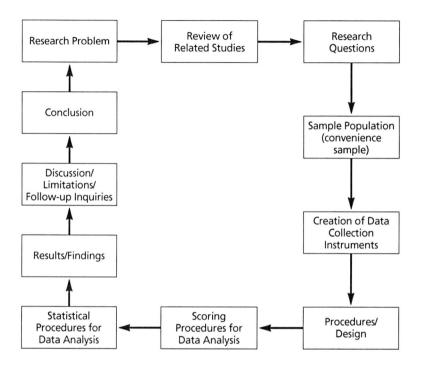

Figure 1.1 The Research Process for Investigations concerning L2 Reading Comprehension Modified from the "General Research Processes in Educational Research," Fraenkel & Wallen, 1996.

both descriptive and inferential, that will be used to analyze the data. Results are then reported and followed by an interpretation of what the findings imply for theory or practice. The discussion includes generalizations and suggestions for follow-up inquiries, and some authors take into account the limitations of the investigation. Finally, a succinct conclusion is offered.

QUALITATIVE INQUIRY IN L2 READING

Qualitative inquiry is concerned with understanding the phenomenon from the readers' perspectives through participation in the learning environment of the reader. Many qualitative studies are ethnographic and aim to understand the L2 reading experience. The researcher becomes immersed in the phenomenon in order to provide a depiction with sufficient detail to show that the author's conclusion makes sense. Discussion of procedures is not emphasized, as the researcher does not have a set agenda. As the data emerges, the researcher begins to draw connections and patterns.

In L2 reading research, qualitative methods are suited for grasping the complexity of the phenomenon investigated. The researcher does not specify before data collection what exactly is being examined. There is an unlimited amount of time devoted to exploring the phenomena, and there is no limit to what will be uncovered. Data collection may include participant observation, collection of documents, and interviewing. Triangulation (either by data, methodology, or investigator) is important in order to search for convergence, inconsistencies, or contradictions. Because qualitative inquiry focuses on the ordinary complexity of L2 reading, it may find what quantitative research is likely not to see. Like quantitative inquiry, the qualitative researcher must ground the interpretations in data. Concepts and categories are clearly exemplified with data from the analysis. Alternative interpretations as well as limitations are often recognized and discussed. Finally, the interpretation is linked to research and theory in L2 reading.

CONCLUSION

The main concentration of this book is on empirical evidence: justification for assertions about L2 reading with adults. The authors share a commitment to examining and understanding the complexity of L2 reading. As a final point, the Editor wishes to thank all the authors and referees for their contributions and cooperation in making this book possible.

REFERENCES

Bernhardt, E. B. (1991). *Reading development in a second language: Theoretical, research and classroom perspectives.* Norwood, NJ: Ablex.

Bernhardt, E. B. (2000). Second-language reading as a case study of reading scholarship in the 20th century. In M. L. Kamil, P. B. Mosenthal, P. D. Pearson, & R. Barr (Eds.), *Handbook of reading research* (Vol. III, pp. 793–811). Hillsdale, NJ: Erlbaum.

Bernhardt, E. B. (2003). New directions in reading research: Second language perspectives. *Reading Research Quarterly, 37*(4), 112–117.

Carr, T. H. (1982). What's in a model: Reading theory and reading instruction. In M. H. Singer (Ed.). *Competent reader, disabled reader: Research and application* (pp. 119–140). Hillsdale, NJ: Erlbaum.

Fraenkel, J. R., Wallen, N. (1996). *How to design and evaluate research in education.* New York: McGraw Hill.

Rayner, K., & Pollatsek, K. (1989). *The psychology of reading.* Englewood Cliffs, NJ: Practice Hall.

CHAPTER 2

THE EFFECTS
OF INPUT FREQUENCY,
TEMPORAL INDICATORS,
AND PRE-READING
QUESTIONS ON L2 READING
COMPREHENSION

James F. Lee and Donna Binkowski

ABSTRACT

The present study examines the comprehension of Spanish future tense morphology while reading in a second language. The participants in the present study had no previous knowledge of future tense morphology such that, as they read the passage used in the study, they encountered the target form for the first time, which is an accented *á* on the end of the infinitive—for example, *dependerá* "he, she, or it will depend." These subjects are a subgroup of those reported on in Lee (2000a). They were given multiple-choice comprehension questions as a pre-reading task in order to orient them toward the meaning of the passage. The independent variables manipulated were (a) the frequency with which the target form appeared in the input passage (6, 10, or 16 exposures), and (b) cues to meaning (the presence or absence

Crossing Languages and Research Methods, pages 7–30
Copyright © 2009 by Information Age Publishing
All rights of reproduction in any form reserved.

of future-oriented adverbials). The dependant variable was the number of multiple-choice questions answered as future meanings. Because subjects performed the multiple-choice task twice, we used a repeated measures design. Comprehension was measured with a multiple-choice comprehension test, administered before and after reading the passage. In addition to the quantitative analyses, we performed qualitative analyses. The results indicate that all the variables have some effect on comprehension.

INTRODUCTION

The Spanish morphological future tense can be described structurally through morphemes: temporal base morpheme, thematic vowel, time/aspect morpheme, and person/number morpheme (Bull, 1963; Stockwell, Bowen, & Martin, 1965; Teschner & Castro, 1993). Table 2.1 shows such a structural analysis for the three verb classes of Spanish in the third-person-singular future tense.

This structural analysis proves a useful tool for describing why the characteristics of Spanish morphological future tense are ideal for empirical examinations of the intersection between two sets of acquisitional processes: learner's processing of meaning (i.e., propositional content) and their processing of form-meaning connections (i.e., the linguistic forms that encode meaning).

The third-person-singular Spanish morphological future tense is formally consistent across all three verb classes. There are no variations in temporal base, thematic vowel (within verb class), nor, importantly, in the morpheme that indicates (i.e., means) future time. In addition to its formal consistency, the time/aspect morpheme of the future tense is orthographically marked and is therefore perceptually salient in written form. Since the orthographic marker indicates the stressed syllable, the form is also perceptually salient in speech. The third characteristic of Spanish morphological future that makes it ideal for empirical examination is its potential to be either of high or low communicative value (VanPatten, 1996, 2003). When a future-tense form is of high communicative value, the form alone is the only temporal indicator in a sentence. When a future-tense form is of low

TABLE 2.1

Temporal base	Thematic vowel	Time/aspect	Person/number
depend	e	rá	∅
practic	a	rá	∅
influ	i	rá	∅

communicative value, the form is redundant with other sentence elements as an indicator of future time. Note the different between the following sentences.

1. *Participará en el torneo de básquetbol.*
   He will participate in the basketball tournament.
2. *Participará el jueves que viene en el torneo de básquetbol.*
   He will participate in the basketball tournament next Thursday.

In sentence 1, the morpheme—*rá* uniquely contributes to future time meaning, whereas in sentence 2, the adverbial, *el jueves que viene*, renders the morpheme redundant. Learners prefer assigning future time meaning via the adverbial over the morpheme (VanPatten's 2003 Temporal Preference Principle). This preference creates an acquisitional challenge for learners: How do learners come to connect the form—*rá* with future meaning when they prefer to use lexemes to establish future time? The present study examines the effects of various factors on learners' comprehension of future time and connection of the morpheme—*rá* to future time.

COMPREHENSION: MAKING MEANING

We define comprehension as making meaning from the propositional context of a text (Lee & VanPatten, 1995/2003). Bernhardt (1991) presents a consensus definition of the comprehension process: Comprehension involves relating new or incoming information to information already stored in the memory. These two related perspectives are supported by empirical investigations of second language reading.

Second-language readers make incoming information conform to an early-instantiated content schema. By analyzing recall, Bernhardt (1991) found many L2 readers who, at the outset of a passage, miscomprehended the German word for "wasteland" as "desert." The result was that they interpreted the entire passage as being about a man in the desert rather than a man wandering the wasteland rubble of war-torn Berlin. Incoming information was made to conform incorrectly to a desert scenario. Lee (1990) found that many L2 readers who had never studied the Spanish preterite tense interpreted (recalled) correctly the events of a passage that began "Between the years 900 and 1000. . . ." Incoming information was made to conform correctly to a past temporal framework.

Second-language readers appear adept at using the temporal base of a verb to assign temporal meaning and are not encumbered by unknown verb endings. Lee (1987) found no differences in comprehension, as measured with recall and open-ended questions, of the specific passage content encoded with the Spanish subjunctive mode between learners who had or had not studied subjunctive forms. Lee (1998) found no differences in passage comprehension (recall) across different versions of the same passage, the three versions being a passage with a correctly conjugated verb form substituted in the other versions by an infinitive or an invented form (-u). Even though the form did not affect comprehension, learners could identify the forms they were exposed to during a post-reading form-identification assessment task. It appears that VanPatten's Temporal Preference Principle (2003) operates not only at the sentence level but also at the word level, especially when learners' task is to make meaning.

INPUT PROCESSING: MAKING FORM-MEANING CONNECTIONS

As noted above, an acquisitional challenge facing learners is not only to make meaning of propositional content but also to connect meaning with the forms that encode it. For example, second-language learners of Spanish must process syllable-final stressed—*ó* as an indicator of past (e.g., *pasó*) and not rely on a past-discourse context only (e.g., "Between the years 900 and 1000....").

Research on second-language acquisition has shown that learners can, at the same time, make both meaning and form-meaning connections (see reviews in VanPatten, 1996, 2003, 2004). Both sets of processes can be engaged simultaneously. While most acquisition research has focused on input delivered aurally to learners, an emerging line of investigation has shown that learners can make meaning [as evidenced in recalls (Lee, 2002a,b; Leeser, 2002) and multiple-choice questions (Lee, 2002a,b; Leeser, 2002; Leow, 1998)] and simultaneously make form-meaning connections [as evidenced in form recognition tasks (Lee, 2002a,b; Leeser, 2002; Leow, 1998) and form production tasks (Lee, 2002b)] through comprehending written input, i.e., through reading in a second language.

THE PRESENT STUDY

The present study analyzes a subset of data presented in Lee (2002a), specifically, the data provided by subjects who performed a meaning-oriented pre-reading task. In the original study, subjects were provided one of three pre-reading orientations: form, meaning, or neutral. These who received the form orientation were informed that they would encounter in the passage they were about to read words that ended in—*á*. They were directed to place a check mark over such words they encountered. Those who received the meaning orientation were provided multiple-choice comprehension questions prior to reading. They were directed to answer each question (guessing what they had to) and then, while reading, verify their answers. The specific wording of the meaning-orientation direction is given in the Appendix A. Those who received a neutral orientation were simply directed to read the passage. In all three orientations, subjects were made aware that after they read, they were to perform a series of post-reading tasks. The results for orientation revealed that immediately after reading the passage, those with meaning orientation recalled significantly more of the target verbs than those with form and neutral orientations. There was no significant difference in recall of target verbs between the form- and neutral-orientation groups. In other words, a meaning orientation enhanced recall of target forms, whereas the form and neutral orientations did not. The results also revealed that immediately after reading the passage, those with a form orientation recognized significantly more of the target verbs on a multiple-choice form recognition test than those with meaning and neutral orientations. There was no significant difference in the number of forms correctly recognized between the meaning- and neutral-orientation groups. In other words, a form orientation enhanced form recognition, whereas the meaning and neutral orientations did not. Given those two findings regarding orientation, we decided to perform further analyses focused on a specific group. We focus the present study on the meaning-orientation group, since their pre-reading task was devised to orient them toward the content of the passage. Although in Lee (2002a) no analysis of learners' performance on the pre-reading question is offered (if learners completed the assigned task, they were included in that study), it is essential in the present study.

Similar to the original study, two independent variables are being addressed in the present analyses in order to specify the effects of pre-reading questions on comprehension. Those variables are Input Frequency and Temporal Indicators. The variable of Orientation is not a factor in the present study, because the data from only one group of learners are being analyzed (i.e., the meaning-oriented group). The research questions guiding this study are:

1. What effect do pre-reading questions have on comprehending future-tense meanings that L2 learners encounter for the first time in a reading passage?
2. What effect does the frequency with which future-tense verb forms appear in a reading passage have on comprehending future tense meanings by learners who answer pre-reading questions?
3. What effect does the presence or absence of temporal indicators in a reading passage have on the comprehending of future-tense meanings by learners who answer pre-reading questions?

In addressing all three questions, comprehension is assessed by comparing readers' performance on the pre-reading multiple-choice questions with their performance on the post-reading multiple-choice questions. Since both sets of questions are identical, comprehension is treated as a repeated measure (Time) in the statistical analysis.

METHOD

Subjects

The Lee (2002a) study began with 283 subjects, all of whom were enrolled in either second-semester Spanish or in the review of a first-year Spanish course at Indiana University. Approximately two weeks before gathering data, the subjects performed a 24-item verb conjugation test, which was used to screen students. They were asked to conjugate six verbs in the first person singular form in the present indicative, preterite, subjunctive, and future. Only those subjects who indicated absolutely no knowledge of the future tense forms were included in the study. For example, we excluded any subject who wrote even a single future form that had an accent mark on it.[1] Of the 181 subjects on whose data statistical analyses were performed, 44 were randomly assigned to receive pre-reading questions as a device for orienting their reading toward the meaning expressed in the passage. The performance of those 44 subjects on the pre- and post-reading multiple-choice comprehension questions is the focus of present study.

Materials

All subjects were provided a separate information sheet regarding the study that informed them that this research involved comprehension and second-language acquisition. All subjects then received a packet of materials. They first encountered one of the three orientations. They then encountered a version of the passage. The passage used in this study was adapted from an authentic text, *El hogar electrónico*, which appears in the students' regular textbook, *¿Sabías que... ? Beginning Spanish* (VanPatten, Lee, & Ballman, 2000). Three versions of the text were prepared such that the texts contained 6, 10, or 16 future-tense verb forms. The passage used in the 6-exposure condition is provided in Appendix A.

Then, for each of these three texts, two versions were constructed. One contained adverbs as additional cues to meaning, and the other did not. Although in Lee, Cadierno, Glass, and VanPatten (1997) each of the seven target forms was accompanied by an adverb, when Lee (2002a) created a version of the 16-target forms passage that included an adverb for each of the 16 forms, the resulting passage read in a most unauthentic way; the discourse was stilted. Since Lee (1990, 1999) found that readers create a general temporal framework, we decided to place adverbs strategically throughout the passages—in particular, at the beginnings of paragraphs.

Assessment Tasks

Lee (2002a) assessed learner/readers' comprehension of what they read as well as their processing of the input for future-tense morphology. Two measures of comprehension were used: free written recall and multiple-choice questions. Both measures of comprehension were taken in the subjects' native language, English, so that their indication of the meaning of what they read would not be obfuscated by their limited L2 systems (Lee, 1987; Shohamy, 1984; Wolf, 1993) and, more important, so that the measures of meaning would be independent of the measures of form. Immediately after reading the passage, learner/readers were asked to write in English everything they could remember from the passage. They were encouraged to write as much as they could. Those recall data are not used in the present study.

Following the recalls, the learner/readers completed multiple-choice questions in English. Each question had a blank in it, and underneath the sentence the learner/readers found four choices. Each blank corresponded to a target verb. The choices rendered the verb in the past, present perfect, present, or future. The correct answer to each question was the future tense of a target verb, and it should be noted that the future choice was distributed among (a), (b), (c), and (d) options. If learner/readers wished to employ a "same-tense" selection strategy, they would have had to search for that particular tense. Because the same multiple-choice questions were used as the pre-reading questions, in the present study we treat the dependent variable, comprehension, as a repeated measure.

Procedures

For Lee (2002a) we prepared packets of materials for each combination of the three independent variables ($n = 18$). The packets were randomly distributed to subjects in their regular classrooms during regularly scheduled classes. For the present study, then, we can say that the 44 subjects we analyzed were randomly assigned to the meaning orientation.

RESULTS

Statistical Analyses

We scored both the pre- and post-reading multiple-choice questions for the number of times a learner selected a future meaning. We refer to the pre-reading scores as Time 1 and the post-reading scores as Time 2. Because we had different input frequencies that yielded different denominators, we converted the scores to percentages before performing a repeated-measures Analysis of Variance (ANOVA) with Temporal Indicators and Input Frequency as independent variables, and Time as the repeated-measure dependent variable. Mean scores, standard deviations, and standard error terms are presented in Table 2.2.

These data were submitted to a $3 \times 2 \times 2$ repeated-measures Analysis of Variance, the results of which are presented in Table 2.3. There were main effects for Input Frequency and Time but not for Temporal Indicators, and there were no significant interactions. We performed a Fisher's Protected Least Significant Difference test (see Appendix B) on each of the variables, the results of which are presented in Table 2.4.

The results of the repeated measures ANOVA showed significant main effects for Input Frequency and Time. There was no main effect found for Temporal Indicators, nor were there any significant interactions. The results of the Fisher's test support and help specify these effects. The test results showed that learners who encountered 6 future-tense forms in the input comprehended significantly fewer future meanings than either learners who encountered 10 ($p = .0002$) or 16 forms ($p = .0009$). Learners who encountered 10 future forms comprehended as many future meanings as those who encountered 16 ($p = .8910$). The test results also showed that learners comprehended more future meanings after reading the passage than they did before reading it. Together, these results indicate that as a

TABLE 2.2 Means, Standard Deviations and Standard Errors for the Variables Time, Input Frequency and Temporal Indicators

Variable		Count	Mean	Std. Dev.	Std. Err.
Time	1	44	37.25	23.32	3.52
	2	44	48.75	32.62	4.92
I F	6	36	26.33	27.03	4.51
	10	30	55.00	23.01	4.20
	16	22	53.91	26.01	5.55
T I	+Adv	46	38.87	30.32	4.47
	–Adv	42	47.52	26.62	4.11

TABLE 2.3 Results of the ANOVA

ANOVA Table for Pretest–Posttest	DF	Sum of squares	Mean square	F-value	P-value	Lambda	Power
Temporal indicator	1	2.906	2.906	.004	.9521	.004	.050
Input frequency	2	15268.377	7634.189	9.623	.0004	19.247	.981
Temporal indicator × Input frequency	2	730.374	365.187	.460	.6345	.921	.117
Subject(group)	38	30144.990	793.289				
Category for Pretest–Posttest	1	2677.756	2677.756	5.207	.0282	5.207	.599
Category for Pretest–Posttest × Temporal indicator	1	1526.692	1526.692	2.969	.0930	2.969	.374
Category for Pretest–Posttest × Input frequency	2	719.493	359.747	.700	.5031	1.399	.155
Category for Pretest–Posttest × Temporal...	2	28.829	14.414	.028	.9724	.056	.054
Category for Pretest–Posttest × Subject(group)	38	19542.341	514.272				

TABLE 2.4   Results of Fisher's PLSD

	Mean difference	Critical difference	P-value
+adv, −adv	−8.65	12.169	.1581
IF 6, 10	−28.67	14.10	.0002*
IF 6, 16	−27.58	15.43	.0009*
IF 10, 16	1.091	16.00	.8910
Time 1, Time 2	−11.50	9.79	.0225*

result of encountering this new form in the reading passage, learners increased their comprehension of the future meanings and that this effect is enhanced by a greater number of exposures to the forms in input.

More Effects of Input Frequency

Since the questions at Time 1 and 2 are identical, we performed qualitative analyses on the data to determine the overlap in answers across the two administrations of the questions. This analysis will help us address more completely Research Question 1. What effect do pre-reading questions have on comprehending future-tense meanings that L2 learners encounter for the first time in a reading passage?

First, we determined the percent of future-selection carryover from one test to the next. To determine future-selection carryover, we counted the number of questions on which learners selected a future meaning at both Times 1 and 2. We then divided that number by the number of correct future meanings selected at Time 2. By analyzing carryover, we can interpret the extent to which reading the passage confirmed the learners' initial hypothesis about the items. In Table 2.5 we present the percentage of future-selection carryover from Time 1 to Time 2 in terms of input frequency.

These percentages indicate another effect for Input Frequency, consistent with the main effect found in the ANOVA results. Specifically, carryover is enhanced by greater exposure to the target forms. From 6 to 10 exposures, the carryover more than doubles.

In addition to carryover we also examined gains made at Time 2 in selecting future meanings on the multiple-choice comprehension questions. To determine the average gain per input-frequency condition, we counted the increase in the future meanings selected at Time 2 over Time I and divided by the number of subjects. As shown in Table 2.6, we found a pattern of increased gain that coincided with increased exposures. On average someone who was exposed six times to the target form increased future-meaning selection by only 1 item, whereas someone who was exposed six-

TABLE 2.5 Percent of Future-Selection Carryover

IF	Carryover
6	35.17%
10	78.58%
16	76.82%

TABLE 2.6 Average and Relative Gains and Losses in Future Meaning Selection at Time 2 × Input Frequency

	Average gain	Relative gain to IF	Average loss	Relative loss	Yield
6	20/18 = 1.11	1.1/6 = 18.33%	11/18 = .61	.61/6 = 10.19%	18.33 – 10.19 = 8.14%
10	35/15 = 2.33	2.33/10 = 23.33%	14/15 = .93	.93/10 = 9.33%	23.33 – 9.33 = 14.00%
16	48/11 = 4.36	4.36/16 = 27.27%	14/11 = 1.27	1.27/16 = 7.95%	27.27 – 7.95 = 19.32%

teen times to the target form increased future-meaning selection by 4 items. We relativized those gains by dividing the average gain by the number of exposures. Average and relative losses in future-meaning selection were fairly constant across input frequencies. Yet, when we calculate a yield in future meanings by subtracting the losses from the gains, we see a dramatic effect for Input Frequency. The yield in future meanings increases steadily as input frequency increases.

Looking at Table 2.7 we see another effect for Input Frequency. Closer examination of the data allows us to categorize or profile learners' tense selection on the pretest and posttest questions in one of six ways: (a) all future, (b) all present tense, (c) all present and future, (d) present and future with one past, (e) mix of all tenses, and (f) all past and present. The selection profiles (Appendix D) show that for higher input levels, the posttest profiles show improvement. With only 6 exposures, learners appear to have broadened their selection profiles, most especially in the category of mixed-tense selections.

More Effects of Time

The statistical analyses revealed a significant main effect for Time. The mean score for selecting a future meaning prior to reading was 37.25%, whereas after reading it was 48.75%, an increase of 11.5%. Learners select

TABLE 2.7   Selection Profiles by Input Frequency

	6		10		16	
	Pre	Post	Pre	Post	Pre	Post
a.	0	1	0	0	0	1
b.	2	2	0	0	0	0
c.	4	3	5	6	3	5
d.	10	6	5	8	5	3
e.	2	1	5	1	3	2
f.	0	5	0	0	0	0

significantly more future meanings after their initial exposure to future-tense forms through reading the passage than they do prior to reading the passage.

We have examined carryover of future meanings from Time 1 to Time 2 in relation to input frequency. Let us now broaden the perspective and profile learners' overall performance at Times 1 and 2. As noted above, we can categorize learners' tense selection on the pretest and posttest questions in one of six ways: (a) all future, (b) all present tense, (c) all present and future, (d) present and future with one past, (e) mix of all tenses, and (f) all past and present. Table 2.8 indicates that only 17 subjects were categorized the same way at Time 2 as at Time 1.

The numbers indicate instability in profiling, meaning that readers were actively engaging the text and not simply relying on the pre-reading questions. That instability is evident in the performance of those profiled as (c) and (d), i.e., (c) "all present and future," (d) "present and future with one past." The combined number of learners across the two profiles at Time 1 was 32 people, and at Time 2, 33. Of the 33 at Time 2, only 14 were included at Time 1. On the positive side we can say that 17 subjects changed profiles from one that included few future tense selections at Time 1 to a profile that included more future meaning at Time 2. Moreover, 2 learners are profiled as having selected only future meanings at Time 2, while no one is profiled that way at Time 1. Finally, on the positive side we see a reduction in the number of learners who selected a mix of tenses at Time 1 ($n = 10$) and then again at Time 2 ($n = 3$). On the down side, 16 learners moved from a profile containing greater future meaning selection to one containing fewer future selections. Whereas the overall percentage gain was 11.5%, the profiles indicate that there is a great deal of individual variation underlying the comparison of means. Learners use the pre-reading questions in a variety of ways.

TABLE 2.8 Profiles of Learners' Performance on Multiple Choice Questions at Times 1 and 2

	Number of subjects per category		# Subjects who are categorized the same way on the post test as on the pretest
	Time 1	Time 2	
a.	0	2	0
b.	2	2	0
c.	12	14	5
d.	20	17	9
e.	10	4	3
f.	0	5	0

More Effects and Non-effects of Temporal Indicators

Temporal Indicators had a significant effect on learners' performance on both recall and multiple-choice comprehension questions in the full data set of 181 subjects (Lee, 2002a). In the present study of 44 subjects who answered pre- and post-reading questions, we found no significant main effect for Temporal Indicators, nor any interaction between Temporal Indicators and Time that approached a level of significance ($p = .09$). The means involved in the interaction, shown in Table 2.9, demonstrated both why the interaction approached significance and why there was no significant main effect. Although subjects were randomly assigned to the meaning orientation, there appears to be a difference between the way subjects responded to the pre-reading questions. Those who then went on to read the passage with temporal indicators had originally interpreted only 29.87% of the questions as referring to a future time. After reading the passage, their comprehension of future meaning significantly increased to 47.96%. Those who went on to read the passage without temporal indicators originally interpreted 45.43% of the questions as referring to future time. After reading the passage, their comprehension of future meaning increased slightly to 49.02%. We consider the difference in performance on the pre-reading questions to be an anomaly in the data set that prevented a significant main effect from happening. Isolating the difference from Time 1 to Time 2 of those who received temporal indicators, we see that temporal indicators do indeed increase comprehension of future meanings. With no temporal indicators, comprehension of future meanings did not increase through reading.

As with the data on Input Frequency, we decided to further analyze the data on Temporal Indicators. In Table 2.10, we present the percent of fu-

TABLE 2.9   Means and Standard Deviations for Temporal Indicators × Time

	Count	Mean	Std. dev.	Std. err.
+Temporal Indicator, Time 1	23	29.78	23.41	4.89
+Temporal Indicator, Time 2	23	47.96	34.03	7.10
−Temporal Indicator, Time 1	21	45.43	20.76	4.53
−Temporal Indicator, Time 2	21	49.02	31.83	6.95

TABLE 2.10   Percent of Carryover of Future Tense Selections from Time 1 to Time 2 and Average Gains, Losses, and Yield in Future Tense Selection at Time 2 × Temporal Indicator

% of carryover	Average gain	Average loss	Yield
+ adv 59.04%	56/23 = 2.43	14/23 = 0.61	2.43 − 0.61 = 1.82
−adv 60.67%	48/21 = 2.29	24/21 = 1.14	2.29 − 1.14 = 1.15

ture meanings carried over from Time 1 to Time 2, the average gain in future meanings comprehended, and the average loss of future meanings. There is practically no difference between the temporal indicator groups in terms of carryover of future meaning from pretest to posttest, nor in the average number of future meanings gained. The interesting figure is that for the average number of future meanings lost from the pretest to the posttest. Those who did not read the passage with temporal indicators lost almost twice as many future meanings as those who read the passage with temporal indicators. The potential effect that we see for temporal indicators is that, in addition to increasing comprehension of future meanings, they help prevent loss of future meanings.

We present in Table 2.11 the six profiles of how learners responded to the pre- and post-test questions grouped by temporal indicator condition. The pattern in the data is similar to the one presented in Table 2.7 for the entire set of 44 subjects. We essentially see the same pattern for both temporal indicator groups.

Once again, let us focus on those profiled as (c) and (d), i.e., (c) "all present and future," (d) "present and future with one past". Whereas the total number of learners with these profiles at Times 1 and 2 are nearly equal, the figures for the overlap between Times 1 and 2 reveal a certain instability in learners' performance. Only 8 of the 16 who received temporal indicators, and 5 of the 16 who did not, had the same profile at Time 1 as at Time 2. Overall, we see little differentiating effect between temporal indicator conditions. Someone in both conditions selected all future meanings at

TABLE 2.11   Profiles by Temporal Indicator

	+ADV			−ADV		
	Pre	Post	Overlap	Pre	Post	Overlap
a.	0	1	0	0	1	0
b.	1	2	0	1	0	0
c.	4	6	2	8	8	3
d.	10	10	6	9	8	2
e.	7	2	2	3	1	0
f.	0	3	0	0	2	0

Time 2. Subjects in both conditions selected all past and present meanings at Time 2, whereas no one did so at Time 1. The number of subjects who selected a mix of tenses decreased from Time 1 to Time 2 in both temporal-indicator conditions.

DISCUSSION

We frame our discussion by highlighting both its greatest strength and its most obvious limitation. We are discussing a very particular context of reading: learner's initial exposure to an unknown verb form. That verb form, as we point out in the introduction, has particular characteristics: formal consistency and relatively high communicative value. We leave it to future research on other verb forms to extend the scope and generalizability of our findings.

The effect of input frequency is the strongest and most consistent effect we uncovered in the analyses. The statistical analyses revealed that more future meanings were comprehended as a result of greater exposure. The qualitative analyses revealed that readers who had the greater exposure to the future tense forms carried over from the pre-test to the post-test a much greater percentage of future meanings. By completing 10 and 16 pre-reading questions,[2] learners seemed to have developed a better sense of the temporal framework of the passage and used it to their advantage.

Our analyses of the yield (i.e., the offset of losses with gains) in future meanings as a result of reading the passage showed a dramatic effect for input frequency. A bit unexpectedly, some learners comprehended fewer future meanings after reading the passage. Many others, however, comprehended more, and while some gained and lost future meanings from Time 1 to Time 2, the yield in future meanings increases steadily as input frequency increases.

In order to understand more fully the effects of pre-reading questions on comprehension, we profiled the learners' answers on the pre-reading questions according to tenses selected. We then profiled their answers on the post-reading questions and determined the overlap. Each of the profiles we presented in the results section demonstrates the same point: Answering pre-reading questions is not a guarantee of increased comprehension for all readers. Clearly there is an overall gain—specifically 11.5%, from Time 1 to Time 2 but there are losses, too. The data in Table 2.6 suggest another possible effect of input frequency on performance. We note once again that a low number of exposures (6) seems to be insufficient for grasping the future meanings of the unknown forms. With only six exposures, learners' post-reading tense selection profiles broaden, as shown by the increase in the category of mixed-tense selection.

Overall we found that temporal indicators had little differentiating effect between groups in the various analyses. This was certainly the case with the tense selection profiles. Probing the data, we are able to support the idea that we found relative, rather than overall, effects. As performance on the pre-reading questions shows, the +Temporal Indicator group thought that only 30% of the pre-reading questions should be answered with a verb expressing future meaning. After reading, they increased that proportion to 48%. The Temporal Indicator group started at 45% and ended at 49%. This finding allows us to affirm the positive effect lexical temporal indicators have on comprehension. Our analyses of carryover of future meanings from pre- to post-test and yields in future meanings show that another effect of lexical indicators in the reading passage was to help prevent loss of future meanings.

CONCLUSIONS

While we acknowledge the limitations of our study—principally the focus on a single verb form and a single reading passage—the results of the statistical and descriptive analyses of the data allow us to make the following conclusions:

1. With regard to the *effects of Time*, we conclude that reading a passage for meaning is sufficient for second-language readers to make appropriate future meanings from forms they did not know.
2. With regard to the *effects of Input Frequency*, we conclude that the frequency with which a second-language reader encounters an unknown form in the input plays a major role in comprehension. Six exposures are sufficient to comprehend some of the meanings,

but much greater comprehension of the form is found after ten and sixteen exposures.

3. With regard to the *effects of Temporal Indicators*, we conclude that their presence in a reading passage has relative, but positive, effects on the comprehension of the future meanings of unknown verb forms. The presence of temporal indicators also seems to help prevent loss of future meanings from pre- to post-test, thus improving the overall yield in future meanings.

NOTES

1. Lee (2002a) purposefully chose not to use a form recognition test as a screening test in order to make the claim that the subjects' initial exposure to future-tense forms occurred while reading the passage. Shook (1994) used both subjects who did and subjects who did not know the forms he investigated and so used gain scores from pretest to posttest in his analyses. Leow (1997) also used a pretest/posttest design to measure gains in formal knowledge. The studies by Leow and Shook cannot speak to the effects of learners' initial exposure to a form.

2. The version containing 16 future tense forms was considered to be of the maximum length for having subjects complete all experimental tasks within one regular 50-minute class period. The 10- and 6-target form versions were then created. The presence of 16, 10, or 6 target forms is related to how coherent the resulting discourse was rather than an attempt to double or halve subjects' exposure. Varying subjects' exposure to target forms is confounded by varying the text they read. The long version contains the information and forms in the other two versions, but the 6-exposure version is significantly shorter than the 10- and 16-exposure version. Due to this factor and the differences in assessment tests (described below), separate statistical analyses were performed for each exposure condition.

REFERENCES

Bernhardt, E. (1991). *Reading development in a second language.* Norwood, NJ: Ablex.

Bull, W. E. (1963). *Spanish for teachers.* Chicago: University of Chicago.

Lee, J. F. (1987). Input processing and the Spanish subjunctive. *Modern Language Journal, 71,* 50–57.

Lee, J. F. (1990). Constructive processes evidenced by early stage non-native readers of Spanish in comprehending an expository text. *Hispanic Linguistics, 4,* 129–148.

Lee, J. F. (1998). The relationship of verb morphology to second language reading comprehension and input processing. *Modern Language Journal, 82,* 33–48.

Lee, J. F. (1999). On levels of processing and levels of comprehension. In J. Gutiér-rez-Rexach & F. Martínez-Gil (Eds.), *Advances in Hispanic linguistics: Papers for the 2nd Hispanic Linguistics Symposium* (pp. 42–59). Somerville, MA: Cascadilla Press.

Lee, J. F. (2002a). The initial impact of reading as input for the acquisition of future tense morphology in Spanish. In S. M. Gass, K. Bardovi-Harlig, S. S. Magnan, & J. Walz (Eds.), *Pedagogical norms for second and foreign language learning and teaching* (pp. 119–140). Philadelphia: John Benjamins.

Lee, J. F. (2002b). The incidental acquisition of Spanish future tense morphology through reading in a second language. *Studies in Second Language Acquisition, 24,* 55–80.

Lee J. F., & VanPatten, B. (2003). *Making communicative language teaching happen.* New York: McGraw. (Original work published 1995)

Lee, J. F., Cadierno, T., Glass, W. R., & VanPatten, B. (1997). The effects of lexical and grammatical cues on processing past temporal reference in second language input. *Applied Language Learning, 8,* 1–23.

Leeser, M. (2002). *The effects of topic familiarity, mode and processing time on processing Spanish future tense morphology.* University of Illinois at Urbana-Champaign dissertation.

Leow, R. (1997). The effects of input enhancement and text length on adult L2 learners' comprehension and intake in second language acquisition. *Applied Language Learning, 8,* 151–182.

Leow, R. (1998). The effects of amount and type of exposure on adult L2 learners' development in SLA. *Modern Language Journal, 82,* 49–68.

Shohamy, E. (1984). Does the testing method make a difference? The case of reading comprehension. *Language Testing, 1,* 147–170.

Shook, D. (1994). FL /L2 reading, grammatical information, and the input-to-intake phenomenon. *Applied Language Learning, 5,* 57–93.

Stockwell, R. P., Bowen, J. D., & Martin, J. W. (1965). *The grammatical structures of English and Spanish.* Chicago: Chicago University Press.

Teschner, R. V., & Castro-Paniagua, F. (1993). *Lo esencial de la lingüística española.* New York: McGraw-Hill.

VanPatten, B. (1996). *Grammar instruction and input processing: Research, theory, challenges and implications.* Norwood, NJ: Ablex.

VanPatten, B. (2003). *From input to output: A teacher's guide to second language acquisition.* New York: McGraw-Hill.

VanPatten, B. (Ed.). (2004). *Input processing.* Mahwah, NJ: Erlbaum.

VanPatten, B., Lee, J. F., & Ballman, T. L. (2000). *¿Sabías que...? Beginning Spanish* (3rd ed). New York: McGraw-Hill.

Wolf, D. (1993). A comparison of assessment tasks used to measure foreign language reading comprehension. *Modern Language Journal, 77,* 473–488.

APPENDIX A:
Sample Materials for 6-exposures Condition

Passage

The title and the adverbs appear in bold here, but not in what learners read. They were removed from the—Adverb versions. Target verbs are underlined here, but not in the versions learners received.
+Adverb/6

En el futuro
En la próxima década, es decir, **dentro de diez años**, dicen que el 60% de la población de los países desarrollados dependerá de las telecomunicaciones.

Muy pronto en el futuro se practicará el teletrabajo con mucha más frecuencia. El profesional liberal mandará el trabajo a cualquier parte del mundo con las tecnologías telemáticas (teléfono, computadora, fax, la red, etc.).

¿Qué nos espera en el futuro? Algunos sociólogos se preocupan porque, según ellos, todo esto generará aislamiento social e influirá en las necesidades de contacto personal. El hombre, Homo sapiens, se convertirá en el Homo electrónicos.

Multiple-Choice Comprehension Questions

Time 1 Directions.
Read the following questions. The answers to these questions can be found in the passage you are about to read. At this moment, even though you have not read the passage, select an answer to each question so that you get some idea of what might take place in the passage. After you answer the questions, turn the page and read the passage. When you are done with the passage, turn the page again. We have a couple of tasks for you to do. You can now turn the page and begin reading.

Time 2 Directions.
Please answer all of the following comprehension questions by selecting the answer that was given in the passage you read.

1. Sixty percent of developed countries ___ on telecommunications.
   a. will depend   b. already depend   c. do not depend
   d. used to depend

2. Telecommuting or teleworking ___ frequently.
   a. is not practiced   b. is already practiced   c. used to be practiced
   d. will be practiced

3. A professional ___ work to any part of the world using telematic technologies.
   a. already sends   b. can not yet send   c. will send
   d. has been able to send

4. Some sociologists claim that these technologies ___ social isolation.
   a. generate   b. can not generate   c. will generate
   d. have already generated

5. Some sociologists claim that these technologies ___ the human need for personal contact.
   a. will influence   b. already influence   c. can not yet influence
   d. have influenced

6. Man, *Homo sapiens*, ___ Homo electronicus.
   a. is already   b. has become   c. can not become   d. will become

APPENDIX B
Fisher's Protected Least Significant Difference Test
for Table 2.4

Fisher's PLSD for Pretest–Posttest Effect: Temporal Indicator Significance Level: 5%

	Mean Difference	Critical Difference	P-Value
+Adverb, –Adverb	–8.654	12.169	.1581

Fisher's PLSD for Pretest–Posttest Effect: Input Frequency Significance Level: 5%

	Mean Difference	Critical Difference	P-Value	
six, ten	–28.667	14.095	.0002	S
six, sixteen	–27.576	15.430	.0009	S
ten, sixteen	1.091	16.004	.8910	

Fisher's PLSD for Pretest–Posttest Effect: Category for Pretest–Posttest Significance Level: 5%

	Mean Difference	Critical Difference	P-Value	
Time 1, Time 2	–11.500	9.788	.0225	S

APPENDIX C
Means Tables for Pretest–Posttest

Effect: Category for Pretest–Posttest

	Count	Mean	Standard Deviation	Standard Error
Time 1	44	37.250	23.322	3.516
Time 2	44	48.750	32.625	4.918

Effect: Input Frequency

	Count	Mean	Standard Deviation	Standard Error
six	36	26.333	27.030	4.505
ten	30	55.000	23.007	4.200
sixteen	22	53.909	26.009	5.545

Effect: Temporal Indicator

	Count	Mean	Standard Deviation	Standard Error
+Adverb	46	38.870	30.319	4.470
−Adverb	42	47.524	26.621	4.108

Effect: Category for Pretest–Posttest × Temporal Indicator
Split by: Input Frequency
Cell: six

	Count	Mean	Standard Deviation	Standard Error
+Adverb, Time 1	13	20.615	21.535	5.973
+Adverb, Time 2	13	34.462	35.585	9.869
−Adverb, Time 1	5	26.600	18.902	8.453
−Adverb, Time 2	5	19.800	21.707	9.708

Effect: Category for Pretest–Posttest × Temporal Indicator
Split by: Input Frequency
Cell: ten

	Count	Mean	Standard Deviation	Standard Error
+Adverb, Time 1	6	46.667	21.602	8.819
+Adverb, Time 2	6	68.333	24.833	10.138
−Adverb, Time 1	9	50.000	13.229	4.410
−Adverb, Time 2	9	56.667	29.155	9.718

Effect: Category for Pretest–Posttest × Temporal Indicator
Split by: Input Frequency
Cell: sixteen

	Count	Mean	Standard Deviation	Standard Error
+Adverb, Time 1	4	34.250	20.855	10.427
+Adverb, Time 2	4	61.250	23.358	11.679
–Adverb, Time 1	7	53.000	23.889	9.029
–Adverb, Time 2	7	61.857	30.635	11.579

Effect: Category for Pretest–Posttest × Temporal Indicator

	Count	Mean	Standard Deviation	Standard Error
+Adverb, Time 1	23	29.783	23.438	4.887
+Adverb, Time 2	23	47.957	34.033	7.096
–Adverb, Time 1	21	45.429	20.755	4.529
–Adverb, Time 2	21	49.619	31.825	6.945

Effect: Category for Pretest–Posttest × Input Frequency

	Count	Mean	Standard Deviation	Standard Error
six, Time 1	18	22.278	20.470	4.825
six, Time 2	18	30.389	32.409	7.639
ten, Time 1	15	48.667	16.417	4.239
ten, Time 2	15	61.333	27.220	7.028
sixteen, Time 1	11	46.182	23.714	7.150
sixteen, Time 2	11	61.636	26.960	8.129

Effect: Category for Pretest–Posttest × Input Frequency
Split by: Temporal Indicator
Cell: –Adverb

	Count	Mean	Standard Deviation	Standard Error
six, Time 1	5	26.600	18.902	8.453
six, Time 2	5	19.800	21.707	9.708
ten, Time 1	9	50.000	13.229	4.410
ten, Time 2	9	56.667	29.155	9.718
sixteen, Time 1	7	53.000	23.889	9.029
sixteen, Time 2	7	61.857	30.635	11.579

Effect: Category for Pretest–Posttest × Input Frequency
Split by: Temporal Indicator
Cell: +Adverb

	Count	Mean	Standard Deviation	Standard Error
six, Time 1	13	20.615	21.535	5.973
six, Time 2	13	34.462	35.585	9.869
ten, Time 1	6	46.667	21.602	8.819
ten, Time 2	6	68.333	24.833	10.138
sixteen, Time 1	4	34.250	20.855	10.427
sixteen, Time 2	4	61.250	23.358	11.679

APPENDIX D
Selection Profiles on Pre- and Posttest

Subject	Input frequency	Temporal indicator	% Pretest*	% Posttest*	% Future carryover	Gain	Loss
1	6	Y	33/d	33/d	100	0	0
2	6	Y	0/d	0/b	0	0	0
3	6	Y	17/d	0/f	0	0	1
4	6	Y	17/d	0/f	33	0	1
5	6	Y	0/b	50/d	0	3	0
6	6	Y	17/d	83/d	100	4	0
7	6	Y	17/e	0/f	0	0	1
8	6	Y	0/d	100	0	6	0
9	6	Y	17/d	33/d	100	1	0
10	6	Y	17/d	33/c	100	1	0
11	6	Y	17/c	0/b	0	0	1
12	6	Y	83/c	83/c	100	0	0
13	6	Y	33/d	33/d	50	1	1
14	6	N	0/b	50/c	0	3	0
15	6	N	17/d	33/e	1	1	0
16	6	N	50/c	0/f	0	0	3
17	6	N	33/c	0/f	0	0	2
18	6	N	33/e	16/d	50	0	1
19	10	Y	60/e	80/c	100	2	0
20	10	Y	80/c	90/c	100	1	0
21	10	Y	50/c	80/d	80	4	1
22	10	Y	40/e	20/e	50	0	2
23	10	Y	30/e	70/d	67	5	1

(continued)

Subject	Input frequency	Temporal indicator	% Pretest*	% Posttest*	% Future carryover	Gain	Loss
24	10	Y	20/e	70/c	100	5	0
25	10	N	50/e	70/d	80	3	1
26	10	N	50/d	70/d	80	3	1
27	10	N	70/c	40/d	57	0	1
28	10	N	30/d	60/c	100	3	0
29	10	N	50/d	30/d	40	1	3
30	10	N	30/d	0/d	0	0	3
31	10	N	60/c	90/c	100	3	0
32	10	N	50/d	90/c	100	4	0
33	10	N	60/c	60/d	83	1	1
34	16	Y	6/e	88/c	100	13	0
35	16	Y	50/d	63/d	70	2	1
36	16	Y	50/d	63/d	88	3	1
37	16	Y	31/e	31/e	20	4	4
38	16	N	38/e	63/d	100	4	0
39	16	N	50/d	44/c	50	4	3
40	16	N	75/c	88/c	100	2	0
41	16	N	38/d	6/e	17	0	5
42	16	N	63/c	69/c	100	7	0
43	16	N	19/d	63/c	100	7	0
44	16	N	88/c	100/a	100	2	0

* Pre- and Posttest Answer Types:
a = all future
b = all present
c = all present and future
d = present and future with one past
e = mix of all tenses
f = all past and present

CHAPTER 3

FAMILIARITY EFFECTS ON LEXICAL ACCESS DURING L2 WORD READING

Andrew P. Farley and Gregory D. Keating

ABSTRACT

Twenty-nine less-fluent readers from a second-semester Spanish course read words and category names in English or Spanish. Readers' reaction times were recorded for their categorization of words during two intra-lingual and two inter-lingual conditions. Statistical analyses reveal no significant difference between the Spanish-Spanish condition and the Spanish-English condition, and no difference between the two intra-lingual conditions. The results indicate that less-fluent readers were able to conceptually mediate while reading and categorizing L2 words. The authors suggest a revised view of an L2 learner's progression from word association to concept mediation. Instead of looking at lexical access during word-level reading in terms of less-fluent and more-fluent learners, it may be more accurate to see the type of lexical access as correlated with the degree of familiarity of the lexical items themselves and as independent of the general notion of a reader's level of proficiency.

Crossing Languages and Research Methods, pages 31–46
Copyright © 2009 by Information Age Publishing
31

INTRODUCTION

Although some L2 reading studies have investigated the processes involved in recognizing form and retrieving concepts at the word or phrase level (e.g., Dufour & Kroll, 1995; Fender, 2003, among others), the majority of L2 reading research has focused on reading at the discourse level (e.g., Lee, 2002; Leow, 1997, McNeil, 1984; Rott, 2000; Rumelhart, 1977, among many others). Current research has primarily sought to both examine and articulate the analytical processes that interact during comprehension of written discourse. While study of the mental processes (activation of schemata, for example) involved during reading at the sentence- and discourse-level is indispensable, a more fundamental research question is the following: *What is occurring at the word-level?* Research on lexical access during word-level reading categorization tasks has thus far been primarily limited to examining the reaction times of relatively proficient bilinguals. Faster reaction times while reading and categorizing words lends support to the theoretical notion that concept mediation (direct form-concept links) is occurring, while relatively slower reaction times may be seen as evidence that learners are word associating ("translating in their heads"). The present study, unique in its focus on very low-level learners, examines what may be happening in L2 readers' minds while performing a word-level comprehension and subsequent categorization task.

L2 LEXICAL ACCESS: THEORETICAL FRAMEWORKS AND RESEARCH

Research on L2 learners' memory representation debates the degree to which proficiency in a second language (L2) determines a learner's ability to access conceptual memory when reading L2 words. Cogent arguments couched in three models of lexical processing have been marshaled for and against the hypothesis that novice and proficient bilinguals process words similarly. The *word association model* holds that L2 words are connected directly to first language (LI) words, and that the L1 lexicon mediates any relationship L2 words have with concepts (Potter, So, von Eckardt, & Feldman, 1984). The *concept mediation model* maintains that L2 words, like their Ll counterparts, have a direct link to conceptual memory (Potter et al., 1984). Kroll and Sholl (1992) specify directional asymmetry between the Ll and the L2, suggesting that L2-L1 translation is accomplished by word association, whereas L1-L2 translation involves concept mediation. A *revised hierarchical model* (Kroll & Stewart, 1994) purports an evolution from word association in the initial stages of L2 word reading (and listening) to concept mediation as the level of fluency rises.

Contention about how bilinguals of varying proficiencies process words in their nonnative language began most notably with the work of Potter et al. (1984). In their study, highly proficient Chinese-English bilinguals performed a translation or picture naming task, or a categorization task requiring participants to match a target word or picture (e.g., dress) to a category name (e.g., clothes). Fluent bilinguals named pictures (which were assumed to have direct access to conceptual memory) in English as fast or faster than they performed Chinese-English word translations, and they categorized pictures in English faster than English words. Potter et al. (1984) replicated the results with a group of less proficient English-French bilinguals who had studied two to three years of high school French. The findings from both groups bolstered support for the concept mediation model of lexical processing across proficiency levels.

Contrary to Potter et al. (1984), Kroll and Curley (1988) and Chen and Leung (1989) found evidence to support two distinct patterns of L2 lexical processing for novice and proficient L2 learners. Speculating that Potter et al.'s (1984) novice learners had already passed a stage of L1 lexical mediation, Kroll and Curley (1988) tested less-fluent and more-proficient English-German bilinguals using word and picture naming tasks. Their beginning learners had less than 30 months of experience, and the more-fluent L2 learners had 30 or more months of experience. The more-proficient group yielded results consistent with the concept mediation model in that they named pictures as fast or faster than words in the L2. The less-fluent bilinguals named words faster than they named pictures, indicating that they relied on first language mediation. Chen and Leung's (1989) proficient Cantonese-English bilinguals and beginning Cantonese-French bilinguals performed similarly to Kroll and Curley's (1988) participants on analogous tasks. The more-proficient learners directly accessed the meaning of words in the L2, while it was concluded that the less-proficient group accessed the L2 words via the L1 lexicon. In both studies, the authors claimed that the level of proficiency determined the pattern of lexical processing.

A peculiar finding in the Kroll and Curley (1988) study led Kroll and Stewart (1994) to propose a revised hierarchical model of lexical representation. Kroll and Curley (1988) predicted that more-fluent bilinguals, being concept mediators, would benefit from translating words that were categorized instead of randomized. However, semantic categorization produced an interference effect; proficient bilinguals translated randomized word lists faster than semantically categorized lists. Kroll and Stewart (1994) replicated the category interference effect with proficient Dutch-English bilinguals. Further experimentation indicated that translation from L1 to L2 required concept mediation and took longer than L2-L1 translation, which was lexically mediated. L1-L2 translation was sensitive to semantic context (categorized vs. randomized) while L2-L1 translation was not. From these

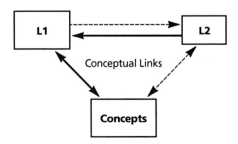

Figure 3.1 The Revised Hierarchical Model of Kroll and Stewart (1994).

conclusions, Kroll and Stewart (1994) proposed the revised hierarchical model of bilingual lexical representation (Figure 3.1).

Sholl, Sankaranarayanan, and Kroll (1995) tested the conclusions of Kroll and Stewart (1994) by using a transfer paradigm to determine whether picture naming during study primes subsequent translation. The revised hierarchical model predicts that picture naming should prime only L1-L2 translation, as this is the only route hypothesized to involve concept mediation. L2-LI translation, which is believed to involve lexical-level processing, should not be primed by previous picture naming. Results from proficient English-Spanish bilinguals support the revised hierarchical model; prior activation of conceptual representations had a positive effect on Ll-L2 translation because it involves concept mediation, but had no effect on L2-L1 translation because it involves lexical association.

While previous research found that concept mediation patterns were a function of language proficiency, Dufour and Kroll (1995) attempted to account for how less-fluent bilinguals are eventually able to mediate the L2 conceptually. They compared the performance of more- and less-fluent English-French bilinguals via a word-level reading categorization task, a context in which conceptual information would be available and perhaps required. Category names and target words were presented in either English or French in four conditions—two interlingual conditions and two intra-lingual conditions. The proficient readers' performance was unaffected by the language of the category name, while the less-fluent word readers had quicker categorization latencies when the language of the category name matched the language of the target word. This finding was significant because it defied prior claims that low-level L2 learners relied exclusively on word-associated processing strategies and provided partial support for Potter et al.'s (1984) results. If novice learners were relying on a simple translation strategy only, the French-French condition would have accrued the longest response times. Dufour and Kroll (1995) had expected the less-fluent word readers to perform the categorization task via word association.

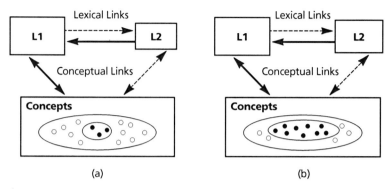

Figure 3.2 Pictorial Representation of Lexicon for (a) Less-fluents and (b) More-fluents (based on Dufour & Kroll, 1995)

However, their results revealed that the novice L2 readers were able to mediate conceptually, although not nearly as well as the more-fluent group. Dufour and Kroll then posited that the strength of the bond between a concept and a lexical item is proportional to one's fluency. As a learner's fluency increases in the second language, they are more able to retrieve lexical items via conceptual activation, not word association (Figure 3.2).

Although the effects of recency and frequency were not formally examined in very low-level learners, Dufour and Kroll (1995) allude to this phenomenon when they state:

> Because it is unlikely that this process is entirely discrete (i.e., individuals do not wake up one morning suddenly able to mediate their second language conceptually), direct concept mediation of L2 must be acquired gradually, *occurring earlier for more familiar words and concepts.* (p. 175; italics added)

Dufour and Kroll acknowledge the natural correlation between familiarity with L2 words and proficiency level. That is, they recognize that as a learner's level of proficiency rises, one's familiarity with words in that L2 also tends to increase.

Word familiarity can be and normally is a function of proficiency level. However, it does not have to be. Generally, the more familiarity learners have with L2 words, the more proficient they are. It is possible, however, that one is quite familiar with a very limited number of words if there is some type of instructional intervention that brings about this scenario. In the present study, the authors are not attempting to pit proficiency level against word familiarity, as if they were always mutually exclusive. Instead, we are simply recognizing that level of proficiency does not have to be high in order for learners to be very familiar with a limited number of words.

Certainly this is not the norm. However, when pedagogical interventions come into play, it is indeed possible for an instructor to purposefully deliver frequent exposure to specific L2 words to learners of relatively low proficiency. In the natural world, it might take a learner X number of hours of exposure to the L2 to hear or read certain words X number of times in a clear context and to assimilate those words into their mental lexicon. In the classroom setting, such exposure can be structured into a curriculum and in a sense "fabricated." This was the case in the present study as learners who were familiar with few L2 words were exposed frequently to a particular subset of L2 words in order to determine whether they might show evidence of concept mediation.

MOTIVATION FOR THE PRESENT STUDY

The common thread in many of the aforementioned studies is the fact that lower-level learners apparently could not approximate the degree of concept mediation found in more-fluent learners. The present study was designed to examine whether very low-level learners with approximately 2.2 years of experience with the L2 (Spanish) can perform as well as or better than Dufour and Kroll's (1995) bilinguals (with an average of 3.9 years of experience) on a word-level reading categorization task if the words tested were both recently and frequently presented to them. The words chosen for the word-reading and categorization task were those which the participants had learned the same semester in which the study took place, whereas in the design of Dufour and Kroll (1995) this was not the case. Given their degree of familiarity with the words, it was hypothesized that these very low-level learners would indeed access conceptual memory to retrieve words, and that their relative performance across conditions would approximate that of a more-fluent learner.

A second motivation for the present study stems from the fact that many of the target words in Dufour and Kroll's (1995) word-reading and categorization tasks were cognates with English. Their less-fluent subjects yielded quicker response times and more accurate responses when cognates were presented in the L2, but no significant difference was found when cognates were presented in the LI. The authors posited that less-fluent L2 learners often bypass concept mediation altogether when the lexical form of the L2 word is similar to that of the L1 word. However, it was difficult to determine whether their subjects were resorting to lexical form comparisons or responding via word association when the L2 category names or words read were cognates. To control for this effect, cognates were entirely avoided in the present study.

RESEARCH QUESTIONS

The present study was designed to answer the following research questions:

1. Will learners of relatively low proficiency show evidence of concept mediation on a word-level reading categorization task when the words have been recently and frequently presented to them?
2. If evidence for concept mediation is demonstrated, will there be any statistical difference in reaction times between the following conditions: Spanish/Spanish, English/English, Spanish/English, English/Spanish?

METHOD

Participants

L2 learners of Spanish with low-level proficiency (second-semester level) were recruited from three intact course sections at a prominent university in the Midwest to participate in the word-level reading study. The mean age of the students participating in the study was 18.89, with approximately 2.2 years of experience with the L2. Participants were enrolled in a second-semester language course that used the textbook ¿Sabías que... (VanPatten, Lee, & Ballman, 1996) as well as the *Destinos* video series (VanPatten, Marks, & Teschner, 1992). Participants received four hours of instruction per week in Spanish, and the rest of their university coursework was carried out in English. Throughout the semester, participants had been presented with both input-based and output-based vocabulary activities involving the lexical items in the present study. Based on the textbook materials and the assignments given in and out of class, it was estimated that participants heard or read each word approximately 811 times and produced (at least in written form) each word 4–6 times. Those figures take into account exact tallies of the individual word occurrences in the written materials used during instruction and an estimate of the tokens produced by both instructor and students based upon those written materials.

Information was collected from each participant about their daily language experiences at home, including which language(s) they spoke at home. Participants that knew more than one second language or had contact with Spanish outside of class were excluded from the study. In addition, all participants who were not native speakers of English or reported any learning disabilities or hearing impairments were removed from the data pool. The final data pool consisted of twenty-nine participants. These participants received credit in the form of extra participation points for volunteering to take part in the study.

Design and Procedure

Participants were required to perform a word-level reading and categorization task in which the category names and the target words appeared in either English or Spanish. The four conditions and some examples are shown in Table 3.1. In the intra-lingual conditions, the category name, and the target word were presented in the same language (i.e., English-English or Spanish-Spanish). In the inter-lingual conditions, the category name and the corresponding target were each presented in different languages (i.e., English-Spanish or Spanish-English). Participants were tested in all four language conditions in separate blocks during a twenty-minute session. The presentation order for the four conditions was randomized according to a Latin square design. L2 learners read eight test categories (vegetables, body parts, places, pets, weather, feelings, jobs, and dining). Each of the test categories included eight target words and eight filler words so that half of the trials required a "yes"-response and half of the trials required a "no"-response. The test categories and target words are listed in the Appendix.

The experiment was run using the DisplayMaster (DMASTR) software developed at Monash University and at the University of Arizona by Kenneth I. Forster and Jonathan C. Forster. DisplayMaster is a group of interrelated MS-DOS software programs written in TurboC and Fortran IV used to display alphanumeric or graphics material for reaction-time experiments

TABLE 3.1 Intralingual and Interlingual Conditions for the Categorization Task

		Language			Response	
		Category	Target	Category	Positive	Negative
intralingual conditions		English	English	vegetable	Peas	bed
		Spanish	Spanish	trabajo	abogado	pluma
interlingual conditions		English	Spanish	Place	Casa	vino
		Spanish	English	mascota	Dog	light

on an IBM-compatible computer. The participants were seated in front of a computer terminal that presented them with category names and target words on the screen. The "Shift" key on the left side of the keyboard functioned as the "no" button, while the "Shift" key on the right side served as the "yes" button. A trial consisted of participants reading a category name that was presented for 250 msec and then reading a target word presented for 300 msec. There was a stimulus onset asynchrony (SOA) of 650 msec between the presentation of the category name and the presentation of the target word. Participants were asked to respond as quickly and as accurately as possible by indicating whether the target exemplar that they read was a member of the previously displayed super-ordinate category. The "yes"-response times (RTs) were measured to the nearest millisecond, while the "no"-responses were disregarded.

RESULTS

Mean categorization latencies for each language condition are presented in Table 3.2. An ANOVA performed on the reaction times ($p = .02$) revealed at least one significant difference among the response times for the four language conditions. Results of the ANOVA for Language Condition are presented in Table 3.3.

Tukey's honestly significant difference (HSD) was calculated to determine which pairs of conditions were significantly different. HSD functions in the following manner: If the absolute difference between two means exceeds the HSD value, then that difference is determined to be statistically significant. The number of observations (29) was the same for each

TABLE 3.2   Mean Categorization Latencies for Each Condition

Condition	Category	Target	Example	RT (MSEC)
1	Spanish	Spanish	lugar / biblioteca	917.59
2	English	Spanish	job / consejero	942.50
3	Spanish	English	mascota / cat	863.91
4	English	English	vegetables / pea	840.16

TABLE 3.3   ANOVA Results for Categorization Task

Source	df	SS	MS	F-ratio	F-critical	p
lang. Condition	3	213,716.15	71,238.12	3.34	2.71	.02
Error	84	1,792,315.34	21,337.09			

TABLE 3.4   Table of Paired Mean Differences (Upper Triangular)

	E-E	S-E	S-S
E-S	102.35	78.60	24.91
S-S	77.43	53.69	
S-E	23.75		

language condition, and the HSD value in this case remained constant at 91.60. As shown in Table 3.4, the paired mean differences produced the following summary results: Language condition E-S (English-Spanish) had a significantly longer reaction time than language condition E-E (English-English) at $p = .05$. That was the only statistically significant difference between conditions. That is, all mean differences between pairs of language conditions, except for E-S vs. E-E, were found to be statistically similar. Of particular note is the fact that there was no significant difference between the Spanish-Spanish condition and the Spanish-English condition. Equally interesting is the fact that no difference was found between the Spanish-Spanish condition and the English-English condition.

DISCUSSION

With regard to a surface-level ordering of reaction times from fastest to slowest for each condition, the results mirror those of the less-fluents in Dufour and Kroll (1995). A visual comparison of the results of the two studies is provided in Figure 3.3. In both the present study and in Dufour and Kroll (1995), the fastest reading and categorization latencies were recorded when the category and the target were presented in the readers' first language (English), while the slowest reaction times occurred when the category was read in English and the target in the L2. In addition, the results of both studies reveal that the mean categorization latency for the L2-L2 condition was not found to be the slowest. That finding in itself lends support to a refutation of the word association model. If the Spanish-Spanish condition (or French-French condition in Dufour and Kroll's study) had been the slowest, this would have signaled the need to translate both category name and target word before giving a response. Since the Spanish-Spanish condition in the present study was not the slowest, it is posited here that these low-level bilinguals were able to mediate conceptually in the L2. In fact, no statistical difference was found between the Spanish-Spanish condition and the English-English condition.

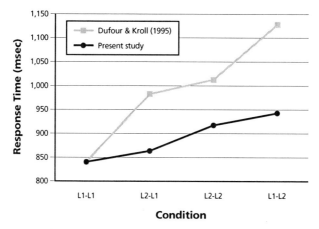

Figure 3.3 Results of present study compared with the Less-fluents in Dafour and Kroll (1995).

For low-level bilinguals to be exhibiting reaction times that are statistically similar for both intra-lingual conditions (E-E and S-S) is more than intriguing. This result begs the question: *Why?* One possible explanation for this result relates to recency and/or frequency effects. Since the words read during the present study were lexical items that had been recently and frequently learned by the participants, they may have been more "familiar" with the words. This might have allowed them to perform the L2 word-reading and a categorization task more quickly than the less-fluents in Dufour and Kroll (1995).

While Dufour and Kroll (1995) concluded that shared conceptual representations may not be activated unless an individual achieves a state of relatively balanced bilingualism, we put forth the idea that it does not *have to be* proficiency in general that strengthens the bond between an individual concept and an individual lexical item. Rather, it is the degree of familiarity that an L2 reader has with an individual word that will determine whether or not they are able to categorize that particular word via concept mediation. That is, a high level of fluency in and of itself does not automatically enable a learner to conceptually mediate, especially if the word(s) involved have not been fully assimilated (i.e., are not very familiar). Similarly, it seems plausible that an early bilingual who has been recently and frequently exposed to a limited number of words would be able to conceptually mediate those words during a word-reading and categorization task due to the high degree of familiarity. We believe this was what was evidenced in the present study.

The present results and the conclusions we draw here should not be interpreted as opposed in any way to what Dufour and Kroll have already stated. Rather, we believe that this study merely lends support to a more finely tuned portrayal of the factors that influence lexical access. We do not view lexical access during L2 word reading as *having to be* a natural progression from word association to concept mediation based on the interdependence of proficiency level and word familiarity. Instead, we posit that the same bilingual might word-associate while reading some words and conceptually mediate when reading others. We argue here that the variation in lexical process is due to the degree of familiarity with each individual word, not to the reader's level of proficiency in general. In agreement with Dufour and Kroll (1995), we acknowledge that in the majority of (natural) cases level of proficiency and word familiarity do have an interdependent relationship. However, when pedagogical intervention occurs, factors such as recency, frequency, and type of exposure may influence how familiar a particular word is and perhaps how that word's meaning is retrieved during reading regardless of a learner's overall proficiency.

Indeed, Dufour and Kroll (1995) acknowledge that "direct concept mediation of L2 must be acquired gradually, occurring earlier for more familiar words and concepts" (p. 175). However, their discussion may be misinterpreted by some to mean that the type of lexical access an L2 learner utilizes is necessarily dependent on some general notion of their proficiency. That is, if one were to label a given number of learners as 'more proficient' or 'less proficient' based upon the general, external evidences exhibited by those learners such as mastery of certain grammatical structures, fluency, pronunciation, etc., then one could accurately predict who conceptually mediates during word reading and who does not. This is precisely where we would choose to express things in a slightly different way to avoid this misconception. Where Dufour and Kroll have pictorially contrasted the less-fluent's lexicon and the more-fluent's lexicon, we would in turn differentiate between the L2 learner who is familiar with few words and the L2 learner who is familiar with many words and leave the term *proficiency* out of the picture.

Since pedagogy and other external factors can intervene, we prefer to entirely divorce the nature of lexical access during word reading from unrelated notions such as mastery of structure, ease of oral production, and other skills commonly associated with the terms *proficiency* or *fluency*. At the same time, we recognize that in the natural world (where no pedagogical intervention has occurred that might alter the situation) there is indeed an observable correlation between level of proficiency and word familiarity. Interestingly, the present study lends support to the idea that the natural relationship between level of proficiency and word familiarity does not *have to be* the case. Consequently, the way in which we talk about concept mediation can be more finely-tuned to include the effects of pedagogical and other interventions that may 'highly familiarize' a low-level learner with certain words.

Familiarity may also be the explanation for the faster reaction times in general (within and across conditions) when compared with the reaction times in Dufour and Kroll's less-fluents. In fact, the reaction times in the present study in many respects more closely resemble the *more proficient* learners in Dufour and Kroll (1995). However, it remains plausible that the slower reaction times among less-fluents in their study were simply due to the use of different computers and different equipment (for example, button boxes as opposed to keyboards). We are not sufficiently informed regarding the electronics used in Dufour and Kroll (1995) to rule out slower circuitry as a possible explanation.

As stated earlier, the results indicate that reaction times for Condition 2 (English-Spanish) are slower than the reaction times for Condition 4 (English-English). Of course, an explanation for this is that the participants benefitted from the 650 msec time period before reading the target stimuli during Condition 3 trials (Spanish-English), but were forced to make decisions immediately after reading a Spanish word in Condition 2 (English-Spanish) trials. That is, when the Spanish appeared last, the categorization latencies were slower because of the weaker relationship between the L2 lexical form and its meaning. However, we question whether the slower reaction times evidenced in Condition 2 indicate that word association was occurring. Is it conceivable that concept mediation occurs at varying speeds within the L2 learner's mind? Do slower reaction times during word-reading and categorization tasks necessarily indicate that word association was utilized? These questions remain unanswered at present.

Future research in this vein of inquiry might include a categorization task that involves *oral production* of a target after a category name is read. Participants' reaction times could be recorded via a microphone attached to a computer terminal. For each block of trials, participants would be told which language to use in their response. For example, in the English-Spanish block, they might read the word "Occupation" and would need to respond as quickly as possible with *abogado* (lawyer) or any other occupation that came to mind. This production-based categorization task would eliminate the need to be familiar with numerous words under a category. Instead, participants would only need to be familiar with the categories they read and could choose their own targets. In this way, even learners with an extremely limited vocabulary could participate in the study.

CONCLUSION

In the present study, L2 learners were able to read and categorize in a statistically similar manner under all conditions except when reading an English category followed by a Spanish target. If these low-level learners had been "translating" (word associating) during the reading and categorization task, then the condition involving the Spanish category and Spanish target would have produced the slowest categorization latencies. However, this was not the case. In the same way that less-fluents in Dufour and Kroll (1995) seemed to possess a limited capacity to conceptually mediate words in their second language, this study has shown that this capacity exists even among very low-level learners. We argued here that a higher degree of familiarity with vocabulary (due to recency and frequency of exposure) was the principal factor determining the nature of lexical processing. In fact, we hold that it is more accurate to say that the degree of familiarity of an individual word (rather than an L2 learner's degree of proficiency) will determine the type of processing that is used during a task that involves reading and accessing the meaning of that word. Therefore, we proposed here an adjusted or more finely tuned view of lexical access during word-level reading. Rather than looking at this phenomenon in terms of less-fluent and more-fluent *people*, word association and concept mediation should be viewed in relation to less familiar and more familiar *lexical items*. When viewing the present study amidst the backdrop of previous research in this vein, we conclude that level of familiarity with individual words may significantly impact the nature of lexical processing during word reading while general level of proficiency may or may not be a correlate.

ACKNOWLEDGMENTS

We would like to thank Robert Dufour and Judith Kroll for their research that inspired the present study. In addition, we acknowledge Giuli Dussias and Susanne Rott, whose courses first familiarized the authors with Display-Master and this vein of research in general. Finally, we would like to express gratitude to the reviewers who gave us insightful feedback and improved the manuscript significantly.

REFERENCES

Chen, H.-C., & Leugn, Y.,-S. (1989). Patterns of lexical processing in a non-native language. *Journal of Experimental Psychology: Learning, Memory and Cognition, 15*, 316–325.

Dufour, R., & Kroll, J. F. (1995). Matching words to concepts in two languages: A test of the concept mediation model of bilingual representation. *Memory and Cognition, 23*,166–180.

Fender, M. J. (2003). English word recognition and word integration skills of native Arabic- and Japanese-speaking learners of English as a second language. *Applied Psycholinguistics, 24*, 289–315.

Kroll, J. F, & Curley, J. (1988). Lexical memory in novice bilinguals: The role of concepts in retrieving second language words. In M.M. Gruneberg, P. E. Morris, & R. N. Sykes (Eds.), *Practical aspects of memory* (pp. 389–395). London: Wiley.

Kroll, J. F., & Sholl, A. (1992). Lexical and conceptual memory in fluent and nonfluent bilinguals. In R. J. Harris (Ed.), *Advances in psychology, Vol. 83: Cognitive processing in bilinguals* (pp. 191–204). Amsterdam: Elsevier.

Kroll, J., & Stewart, E. (1994). Category interference in translation and picture naming: Evidence for asymmetric connections between bilingual memory representations. *Journal of Memory and Language, 33,*149–174.

Lee, J. F. (2002). The incidental acquisition of Spanish future tense morphology through reading in a second language. *Studies in Second Language Acquisition, 24,* 55–80.

Leow, R. P. (1997). The effects of input enhancement and text length on adult L2 readers' comprehension and intake in second language acquisition. *Applied Language Learning, 8,* 151–182.

McNeil, J. D. (1984). *Reading comprehension: New directions for classroom practice.* Glenview, IL: Scott Foresman.

Potter, M. C., So, K.-F., von Eckardt, B., Feldman, L. B. (1984). Lexical and conceptual representation in beginning and proficient bilinguals. *Journal of Verbal Learning and Verbal Behavior, 23,* 23–38.

Rott, S. (2000). Relationships between the process of reading, word inferencing, and incidental word acquisition. In J. F. Lee & A. Valdman (Eds.), *Form and meaning: Multiple perspectives* (pp. 255–282). Boston: Heinle & Heinle.

Rumbelhart, D. E. (1977). Toward an interactive model of reading. In S. Dornic (Ed.). *Attention and performance VI: Proceedings of the Sixth International Symposium on Attention and Performance* (pp. 573–603). New York: Academic Press.

Sholl, A., Sankaranarayanan, A., & Kroll, J. (1995). Transfer between picture naming and translation: A test of asymmetries in bilingual memory. *Psychological Science, 6,* 45–49.

VanPatten, B., Lee J. F., & Ballman, T. L. (1996). *¿Sabías que...? Beginning Spanish* (2nd ed.). New York: McGraw Hill.

VanPatten, B., Marks, M. A., & Teschner, R. V. (1992). *Destinos: An introduction to Spanish* (videocassette series). New York: McGraw-Hill Inc.

APPENDIX
List of Category Names and Target Word

Vegetables / Verduras
onion / cebolla
pepper / pimiento
peas / arvejas
beans / frijoles
rice / arroz
carrot / zanahoria
corn / maíz
artichoke / alcachofa

Weather / Tiempo
cold / frío
heat / calor
wind / viento
sun / sol
clouds / nubes
rain / lluvia
snow / nieve
cool / fresco

Place / Lugar
library / biblioteca
house / casa
church / iglesia
store / tienda
city / ciudad
kitchen / cocina
bedroom / alcoba
country / país

Job / Trabajo
lawyer / abogado
nurse / enfermera
librarian / bibliotecario
salesman / vendedor
writer / escritor
singer / cantante
counselor / consejero
accountant / contador

Body / Cuerpo
hand / mano
arm / brazo
foot / pie
face / cara
eye / ojo
nose / nariz
mouth / boca
hair / pelo

Pet / Mascota
dog / perro
cat / gato
fish / pez
hamster / cuy
monkey / mono
snake / culebra
horse / caballo
mouse / ratón

Feel / Sentirse
bored / aburrido
happy / alegre
tired / cansado
bad / malo
sad / triste
embarrassed / avergonzado
angry / enojado
sick / enfermo

Dining / Cenar
knife / cuchillo
spoon / cuchara
fork / tenedor
napkin / servilleta
table / mesa
glass / vaso
dessert / postre
pitcher / jarra

CHAPTER 4

TOWARD A DEPENDABLE MEASURE OF METACOGNITIVE READING STRATEGIES WITH ADVANCED L2 LEARNERS

Cindy Brantmeier and Boncho Dragiyski

ABSTRACT

In a preliminary investigation, a metacognitive knowledge test entitled NEL-SON (Van Gelderen et al., 2003) was used with advanced L2 adult learners of Spanish at a university in the USA in order to examine the relationship between L1 and L2 metacognitive skills, L2 linguistic knowledge, and L2 reading comprehension. Findings revealed no positive relationship for overall metacognitive knowledge and L2 reading comprehension. With the advanced L2 learners, L2 linguistic knowledge seemed to be a more powerful predictor of L2 reading comprehension than metacognitive skills. Given the findings of this preliminary investigation, a follow-up study was conducted with 129 advanced L2 adult learners of Spanish using Mochtari and Reichard's (2002) Metacognitive Awareness of Reading Strategies Inventory (MARSI). Participants read two different authentic texts (a short story and an essay) and completed three different comprehension assessment tasks: writ-

Crossing Languages and Research Methods, pages 47–72

ten recall, sentence completion items, and multiple choice items for each reading. Regression analysis revealed that certain combinations of metacognitive items on the MARSI positively associate with reading comprehension for specific text types and assessment tasks. For both texts, the same combinations of items provided positive associations for recall but not for sentence completion and multiple choice. Results hold important implications for both instructors and researchers as the MARSI proved to be a dependable measure used with advanced L2 learners. Instructors may want to consider combinations of results when teaching different metacognitive strategies in the classroom. The MARSI questionnaire may also aid instructors to diagnose strengths and weaknesses of individual readers.

INTRODUCTION

Findings across several prior experiments yielded low L2 reading comprehension scores for different assessment tasks with learners from advanced levels of language instruction (Brantmeier 2006a,b; Brantmeier & Vanderplank, 2008). Consequently, there is a strong need for instructors to facilitate the development of reading skills in the classroom. Most researchers agree that metacognition involves the organization, use and monitoring of cognitive activity throughout the reading process—before, during and after reading. Given the importance of metacognition in the L1 reading process, along with the known impact that L1 literacy has on L2 reading, the topic of metacognition and L2 reading is timely and critical. Within existing studies on this subject matter there are great variation and disparity regarding data collection instruments, age of participants, etc., and consequently, it is difficult to make generalizations. To date, it appears that only a few investigations have examined the relationship between metacognition and L2 reading comprehension with advanced learners at a university.

LITERATURE REVIEW

Metacognition and L1 Reading

Many L1 investigations, both qualitative and quantitative, have examined the role of metacognition in reading. Several important reviews of this research have been published (see Baker & Brown, 1984; Brown, 1987a,b, for examples) that indicate the positive effects of metacognition on reading in one's native language, and most of these studies utilize young participants, mainly from elementary school. It is common knowledge that good L1 readers effectively use strategies and skills to process the text, and researchers seem to agree that the effective use of metacognitive strategies and skills could, in part, be due to age and experience (Brown, 1987a,b; Layton, Robinson, & Lawson, 1998; Owings & Petersen, 1980; etc.).

Evidence shows that good learners exhibit higher metacognitive awareness, followed by enhanced learning effectiveness and efficiency, than poor ones (Zimmerman, 1989; Zimmerman & Bandura, 1994; Dickinson, 1995). Romero and Tobias (1996) analyzed "seeking help" as a predictive indicator of metacognitive awareness, suggesting that the L1 learners' capacity to recognize, and the intent to address, a learning problem point toward higher self-monitoring ability. The findings of their study, which includes 41 fourth-grade native speakers of English from urban public schools, suggest that there is a significant positive correlation between the metacognitive knowledge monitoring ability of L1 learners and their literacy level/reading performance. Furthermore, some researchers also establish correlations between metacognitive ability and scholastic aptitude (Tobias & Everson, 2002). By challenging traditional definitions of academic talent and by considering the range of metacognitive awareness of L1 students, the preliminary results obtained by Tobias, Everson, Laitusis, and Fields (1999) broaden the importance of metacognitive knowledge monitoring in the domain of reading by arguing that monitoring ability can be considered "better" for predicting reading success than the prior knowledge of the content to be read. In other words, reading comprehension is not necessarily as important as the L1 students' general monitoring accuracy in learning to read (Tobias & Everson, 2002).

Given the above assertions regarding L1 reading and metacognition, Mokhtari and Richard (2002) developed and validated a self-report instrument, the MARSI, for assessing metacognitive awareness and perceived use of reading strategies for adults while they read L1 academic materials. The instrument was designed and developed after carefully examining the most recent research on metacognition and reading comprehension as well as a thorough review of existing reading strategies instruments. Initially, the instrument included sixty items that were tested with 825 participants (from grades 6–12), and after careful and thorough analysis of items, the questionnaire was reduced to 30 items. The revised instrument was again tested with 443 students of the same ages as previous testing. The result revealed that three factors explained 29.7% of the total variance, and these three factors were categorized as: (1) global reading strategies, (2) problem-solving strategies, and (3) support reading strategies. To provide evidence of construct validity, the authors examined the relationship between self-reported reading ability and strategy use and found that the MARSI is a reliable and valid measure for assessing students' metacognitive awareness and perceived strategy use while reading. Since 2002, the MARSI has been used by L1 practitioners and researchers alike.

Metacognition and L2 Reading

While research on metacognition and L1 reading has received considerable attention for years, there remains a lot to be done with this factor and
L2 reading. After an initial call for more research that attends to metacognitive variables in L2 reading (Carrell, 1989), some studies tended to focus
on cognitive monitoring strategies (see Devine, 1993, for complete review).
See Table 4.1 for a detailed list of selected studies on metacognition and
L2 reading.

In a study that explores reading strategies used by readers in their L1
and their L2, Carrell and Carson (1993) demonstrate that good L1 readers are good L2 readers as well, although not because they use the same
strategies to process reading materials. Findings indicate that native and
nonnative readers perform similarly on cloze tests in a given language, but
differently in different languages. The role of L1 reading comprehension
in explaining L2 reading is also an important issue in van Gelderen et al.'s
(2004) longitudinal study examining Dutch and English reading skills with
students from secondary education. Given the discussion concerning the
conditions of L1-L2 transfer and the contribution of L1 reading comprehension strategies to the construction of L2 reading skills, van Gelderen et
al. concur with Goodman's (1971) hypothesis. They conclude that metacognitive knowledge greatly contributes to both L1 and L2 reading comprehension and that L1 reading comprehension explains a substantial proportion of variance in L2 reading comprehension.

In a comparison of bilingual and monolingual students, Fajar, Santos, and
Tobias (1996) report that bilingual school students more actively monitor
reading comprehension than their monolingual counterparts. Two recent
studies also raise questions about the importance of metacognitive awareness and comprehension monitoring in bilingual and trilingual speakers. In
a 2007 study, Kolić and Bajšanski explore comprehension monitoring, use
of reading strategies, and reading comprehension of bilingual students at
different levels of perceived proficiency in Italian. After using three different sets of measuring instruments, the authors conclude that comprehension monitoring is the most important predictor of reading comprehension
of bilingual students. They also stipulate that significant improvement in
reading comprehension during the higher educational levels beyond the
8th grade could be attributed to improvement in the effectiveness of comprehension monitoring. In another study, van Gelderen et al. (2003) utilize
L1, L2, and L3 readers from secondary education to examine the role of
linguistic knowledge, speed of processing, and metacognitive knowledge in
the L2 reading process. The researchers conclude that the componential
nature of reading comprehension in L1, L2, and L3 are the same, despite
differences in skill level.

TABLE 4.1 Literature Review: Metacognition and L2 Reading

Author and year	Research questions	Participants	Procedures	Results
Carrell 1989	What is the metacognitive awareness of L2 readers about their reading strategies in both their L1 and L2? What is the relationship between metacognitive awareness and reading comprehension in both L1 and L2?	Group 1—45 native speakers of Spanish, studying at Southern Illinois University (English = L2); Group 2—75 native speakers of English, studying Spanish at the same institution (Spanish = L2)	Tested in L1 and L2 sessions. Read two texts in the language in question and answer multiple-choice comprehension questions. Complete a metacognitive questionnaire	For reading in L2, local strategies tend to show negative correlation with the reading performance. With the L1 English group with lower proficiency of Spanish, some local strategies (bottom-up) are positively correlated with reading performance; for the L1 Spanish group, at the higher level of language proficiency in L2, some global strategies (top-down) are positively correlated with the participants' reading performance
Carrell, Pharis, & Liberto 1989	Does metacognitive strategy training enhance L2 reading? Does one type of strategy training facilitate L2 reading better than another? Is there a relationship between the students' learning styles and the metacognitive strategy training?	26 students in level 4 of the intensive program of the Center of English as a L2 at Southern Illinois University. The participants have heterogeneous linguistic backgrounds (Arabic, Japanese, Chinese, Greek, Spanish, and French)	Four-day strategy training was provided to both groups. Read three passages, complete multiple-choice questions, partial cloze semantic map filling, and a self-created semantic map	Results show that metacognitive training (in semantic mapping and in experience-text-relationship) is effective in enhancing L2 reading, and that the effectiveness of one or another type of training depends on the way reading processes are measured. Findings indicate significant interactions between the participants' learning styles and the effectiveness of metacognitive training in the two different strategies

(continued)

TABLE 4.1 Literature Review: Metacognition and L2 Reading (continued)

Author and year	Research questions	Participants	Procedures	Results
Verhoeven 1990	What kind of metacognitive strategies do children use in their L1 and L2 reading processes during the first two grades of school?	74 native speaking children of Turkish, first-graders, living in three cities in the Netherlands (Dutch = L2)	Complete word reading task, reading comprehension task, oral L2 proficiency task, and sociocultural orientation measures. The Raven's Progressive Matrices Test was used to measure nonverbal metacognitive skills	The influence of bottom-up processes of word recognition tends to decrease, and is gradually replaced by top-down strategies, as children become more experienced in their L2. The study also provides evidence of the role of sociocultural orientation in L2 reading acquisition
Carrell & Carson 1993	Do reading strategies vary with language? Are L1 successful strategies responsible for the success in L2 reading comprehension as well?	Group 1—60 native speakers of Chinese, studying at US universities (English = FL); Group 2—28 native speakers of English (monitoring group)	Read two cloze passages, one in Chinese and one in English, with a fixed-ratio random deletion	Three main conclusions emerge from the study's results: 1. Native and nonnative readers perform similarly on cloze in a given language; 2. Readers perform differently in different languages; 3. Native and nonnative students seem to use the same strategies on cloze in a given language
Van Gelderen, Schoonen, Glopper, Hulstijn, Simis, Snellings, & Stevenson 2003	What are the contributions of L1 reading comprehension for readers of L1 and L2? What are the contributions of the components in L2 reading comprehension for readers of L2 as L2 and L3?	397 native speakers of Dutch from grade 8 to grade 10 in secondary education studying English as a FL	Complete reading proficiency test, vocabulary test, grammatical knowledge test, metacognitive awareness questionnaire, lexical decision task, and sentence verification task. All tests had an English and a Dutch version excluding metacognitive questionnaire	The results suggest that contributions of L1 (Dutch) reading comprehension to both L1 and L2 reading are substantial in all instances except in the case of speed word recognition and sentence verification. The contribution of linguistic knowledge to L2 (English) reading comprehension for both L2 and L3 readers of English is also significant, particularly in the case of metacognitive knowledge

Study	Research questions	Participants	Method	Findings
Van Gelderen, Schoonen, Glopper, Hulstijn, Simis, Snellings, & Stevenson 2004	Does metacognitive knowledge explain L1 and L2 reading comprehension? To what extent does L1 reading comprehension contribute to L2 reading comprehension beyond the contributions made by L2 components?	397 native speakers of Dutch from grade 8 to grade 10 in secondary education studying English as a FL	11 different instruments (knowledge and speed tests) were developed	Findings indicate significant contribution of L1 reading comprehension to L2 reading comprehension. Metacognitive knowledge seems to have a large contribution in explaining not only L1 but L2 reading comprehension as well
Brantmeier 2005	How do students at advanced levels of L2 instruction asses their reading abilities? Is there a relationship between self-assessment and enjoyment in L2 reading? Is there a relationship between self-assessment and comprehension?	88 L2 learners of advanced Spanish at a university	Read, complete written recall and multiple-choice task. Questionnaires were used to assess self-assessment and enjoyment levels	Findings reveal a significant relationship between self-assessed L2 reading ability and written recall scores. Self-assessed abilities also show positive correlation with the levels of enjoyment (the higher the level of self-assessment the higher the level of enjoyment in L2 reading)
Bell 2007	What practices and strategies do participants use during their L2 reading? Is there a relationship between reading comprehension and extratextual individual experiences?	Unspecified number of postgraduate students from India and Bangladesh, studying at an Australian English-speaking University	Complete a discipline-specific text and interview about approaches to reading the text. A combination of think-aloud protocols and retrospective interviews	Results suggest that students made significant use of intratextual framing and drew on their personal background knowledge and extratextual experiences where the in-text features were not sufficiently helpful for the understanding of the L2 text. There is a positive relationship between reading comprehension strategies and the student's level of interest and confidence

(continued)

TABLE 4.1 Literature Review: Metacognition and L2 Reading (continued)

Author and year	Research questions	Participants	Procedures	Results
Fotovatian & Shokrpour 2007	What are the effects of different reading strategies on reading comprehension of L2 readers? How do strategies during reading explain good and poor students' reading comprehension?	31 university students whose L1 is Farsi	Complete reading version of the First certificate in English, followed by a questionnaire including a list of 24 strategies categorized into metacognitive, cognitive, and socio-affective	Finidings indicate: skillful readers make use of a larger set of various reading comprehension strategies, use metacognitive strategies more frequently, and have better knowledge of the different reading comprehension strategies than poor readers.
Kolić & Bajšanski 2007	What are the effects of comprehension monitoring and the use of reading strategies in bilingual reading comprehension? Are there developmental differences in reading comprehension, comprehension monitoring, and use of reading strategies at the different levels of perceived language proficiency?	271 students from the fifth to the eight grade in four Italian elementary schools (Italian = L2) in Croatia (Croatian = L1)	Complete three sets of evaluative measures: 1. Assess comprehension monitoring (error-correction test, text sensitivity test, and cloze test); 2. Use of reading strategies; 3. Proficiency use of Italian (15-questions questionnaire)	Comprehension monitoring is the most important predictor of reading comprehension of bilingual students. Comprehension monitoring differs in students with high and low perceived proficiency in Italian, difference attributed to the improvement in the effectiveness of comprehension monitoring in reading comprehension of higher grade students
McKeown & Gentilucci 2007	Which comprehension strategies are the most effective in helping students fill in gaps of their L2 knowledge, especially during reading comprehension? Are all metacognitive strategies equal for all levels of instruction?	27 L2 (English) learners with a reading proficiency of early intermediate or higher, divided in three groups; the students have a diverse and unspecified linguistic background	Complete High Point Comprehension Assessment	Findings suggest that while L2 (English) learners successfully use metacognitive strategies, the efficiency of these metacognitive strategies depends largely on the particular level of proficiency of the students.

Devine (1993) presents an extensive summary of recent research on metacognition and L2 reading and offers possible directions in which this research can enhance understanding of L2 reading. She specifically details Carrell's (1989) study that investigates the metacognitive awareness of L2 readers about reading strategies in both their L1 and L2, and the relationship between metacognitive awareness and reading comprehension in both L1 and L2. Results show that advanced students of ESL tend to use top-down strategies during reading in L2, while lower proficiency levels of Spanish as L2 use bottom-up strategies. Carrell, Pharis, and Liberto (1989) explore the use of metacognitive strategy training for reading in ESL. Their findings suggest that not only is training in metacognitive strategies use beneficial for enhancing L2 reading, but that there is a significant relationship between the students' learning styles and the effectiveness of training in the two different strategies for L2 reading comprehension (semantic mapping and experience-text-relationship).

Recently, McKeown and Gentilucci (2007) turn their attention to those comprehension strategies that are most effective in helping L2 students fill gaps in their meaning-making strategies. The researchers conclude that while L2 learners of English successfully use metacognitive strategies, such as think-aloud protocols, the efficiency of the strategies depends largely on the unique needs of each particular level of proficiency. The authors of the study also suggest that teachers should not make the mistake of considering all strategies as "good" strategies and apply them equally to all levels of L2 learning. Knowledge of the strategies that L2 learners use can certainly help instructors incorporate and teach these techniques in their classrooms in order to enhance the students' reading comprehension. Focusing on metacognitive, cognitive, and socio-affective strategies, Fotovatian and Shokrpour (2007) compare efficiency of strategy use and examine effects on L2 reading. Their categorization follows O'Malley & Chamot's (1990) taxonomy where metacognitive strategies are "higher order executive skills that may entail planning for, monitoring, or evaluating the success of a learning activity" and cognitive strategies "operate directly on incoming information, manipulating it in ways that enhance learning." Socio-affective strategies, on the other hand, involve "interacting with another person to assist learning or using affective control to assist a learning task" (p. 49). Findings suggest that metacognitive strategies have positive effects on L2 reading comprehension; furthermore, skillful readers use a larger number of various reading comprehension strategies while poor readers seldom use any during the reading process.

In an investigation that examines the reading processes of children learning to read in L1 and in L2, Verhoeven (1990) reaches similar conclusions to Carrell's (1989) study with adult students. Verhoeven explores the processes of literacy acquisition of Turkish children learning to read Dutch during the first two grades of primary school. Findings demonstrate that the influence of bottom-up processes of word recognition tends to decrease as children become more experienced in the L2. Additionally, sociocultural factors also influence L2 reading. Brantmeier (2005), with readers from advanced levels of L2 instruction, examines L2 learners' self-assessment of reading abilities and the relationship between self-assessment and enjoyment in L2 reading. The author found a significant relationship between self-assessed L2 reading ability and written recall scores, and the higher the level of self-assessment the higher the level of enjoyment.

Bell (2007) employs various ethnographic procedures in order to understand how L2 students frame and manage their metacognitive abilities to better understand texts. Bell's conclusions show that the participants made significant use of intratextual framing and drew on their individual knowledge and experience to fill those gaps where the in-text features were not sufficient to aid their understanding of the L2 text. Overall, the above review of research on metacognition and L2 reading demonstrates that metacognition is a factor in L2 reading worthy of further examination.

Connections between L1 and L2 Reading

As evidenced by research, metacognition is an important part of L1 literacy, and L2 readers may rely on L1 literacy for metalinguistic functions during L2 reading. Bernhardt and Kamil (1995) investigate whether L2 reading is a language problem or a reading problem. Results show that neither factor is completely reflective of the reading process as both variables are contributors. They state that the contribution of L1 reading performance must be considered when examining the L2 reading process, and naturally metacognition can be considered a part of the L1 reading process. Bernhardt (2005) offers a synthesis of research that analyzes the contribution of L1 literacy and second language knowledge to L2 reading performance. Overall, the studies estimate the contribution of L1 reading to L2 reading to be between 14% and 21% (Bernhardt & Kamil, 1995; Bossers, 1991; Brisbois, 1995; Carrell, 1991). Bernhardt's (2005) model includes both L1 reading and L2 language as factors involved in the multivariate L2 reading process. Her model also underscores the need for more research across languages and levels that takes into account the contribution of L1 reading to L2 reading. The present investigation considers metacognition to be part of L1 reading practices and therefore is part of the L2 reading process.

The Preliminary Study on Metacognition and L2 Reading

In a preliminary investigation, the metacognitive knowledge test entitled NELSON (Van Gelderen et al., 2004), that was developed for secondary students in the Netherlands, was utilized with 98 advanced L2 adult learners of Spanish at a university in the USA. The investigation in the USA examined the relationship between L1 and L2 metacognitive skills, L2 linguistic knowledge (grammar and vocabulary), and L2 reading comprehension. While the study found relationships between linguistic knowledge and L2 reading comprehension, findings revealed no positive relationship for overall metacognitive knowledge and L2 reading comprehension. More specifically, a significant relationship between L2 linguistic knowledge and L2 reading comprehension was found only with an online reading test. With the advanced L2 learners at the university, L2 linguistic knowledge seemed to be a more powerful predictor of L2 reading comprehension than metacognitive skills.

It is important to note that the languages tested were native language English and target language Spanish, and that the participants were more advanced in the educational levels than the participants in the Netherlands experiments. Furthermore, the NELSON tests higher level reading processes, but the students in the preliminary test were poor L2 readers. The advanced learners in the experiment were not advanced readers. Test-method effect of the metacognitive instruments could explain insignificant results with metacognition. Given the initial findings of this preliminary investigation, a follow-up study with advanced L2 adult learners of Spanish using Mochtari and Reichard's (2002) Metacognitive Awareness of Reading Strategies Inventory (MARSI) was conducted. As discussed earlier, the MARSI was originally created for university level students whose L1 was English and has been modified and utilized for L2 learners of English.

THE PRESENT STUDY

For the present study, the MARSI was utilized with advanced adult L2 readers to assess the relationship between metacognitive strategy use and comprehension with two different authentic texts. The following research questions guide the present study:

1. Do self-reported global reading strategies yield a positive association with L2 reading comprehension tasks?

2. Do self-reported problem-solving strategies yield a positive association with L2 reading comprehension tasks?
3. Do self-reported support reading strategies yield a positive association with L2 reading comprehension tasks?

Methodology

Participants

A total of 129 native speakers of English, ages 19–22, participated in the present study. All subjects were enrolled in an advanced level Spanish grammar and composition course at a middle-sized, private, Midwestern university. This third-year course was the first in a two-course sequence taken immediately before entering literature courses, and the course marked the start of the Spanish major or minor. As part of the course students were assigned to read lengthy, authentic literary works from the literary canon. At the university where data was collected there is no language requirement, and therefore all students in the study enrolled in the course voluntarily. Only students with the following criteria were included in the final data analysis: (1) students who achieved the appropriate composite score on an online placement examination (tested into advanced Spanish grammar and composition), (2) students whose native language was English, and (3) only students who completed all tasks.

Reading Passages

The Spanish readings included both a narrative text and an expository text. The first passage was entitled "Una conversación con Rigoberta Menchú" and was a narrative about the childhood of Rigoberta Menchú, a native American from Guatemala. It included approximately 512 words. The passage details Rigoberta's work as a child on the cotton plantations and includes family experiences. The second Spanish passage is an expository text entitled "Television: Cultura y Diversidad" which discusses various perspectives on the role of television in culture and civilization, and it contains about 318 words.

Comprehension Assessment Tasks

Three different assessment tasks were completed to measure comprehension: written recall, sentence completion and multiple choice. Immediately following each passage, the written recall asked the readers to write down in their native language as much as they could remember about each passage. Several reading specialists were consulted concerning the construction of the sentence completion and multiple choice questions. A response for each sentence completion question corresponded to an item in each multiple choice question (Wolf, 1993); therefore, respondents completed the sentence completion before the multiple choice questions. Questions included an overall global comprehension question as well as detail-oriented items. The multiple choice questions had 4 possible answers; the incorrect answers representing plausible distracters. All comprehension assessment tasks were completed in the reader's native language (Lee, 1986; Shohamy, 1982, 1984; Wolf, 1993).

Topic Familiarity

Topic familiarity was assessed via written questions with five possible choices ranging from 1 (I was really familiar with this topic) to 5 (I was not familiar with this topic at all). No significant differences were found by gender for topic familiarity with either reading passage.

Data Collection Procedures

All subjects completed the following instruments in this order during a regular class period of 50 minutes for each reading passage: reading passage, written recall, sentence completion items, multiple-choice questions, and topic familiarity questionnaire. When participants completed the above, they then filled out the MARSI questionnaire.

No details about the experiment were provided to participants other than the fact that they were invited to participate in an experiment concerning L2 reading. No participants declined to participate in the study. The researcher and/or a research assistant along with all instructors for the courses were present during data collection sessions to monitor progress and to ensure that students did not look back at any previous pages while reading and completing all tasks.

Data Analysis

The items on the MARSI were categorized according to the same rubric used by Mochtari and Reichard (2002): global reading strategies, problem-solving reading strategies, support reading strategies and overall reading strategies. These four factors were the independent variables. See Appendix A for a complete list of categorized items used on the inventory for this investigation. Note that for the present study some items from the original MARSI (2002) were omitted as they were not relevant to the passages.

For each reading passage, three different dependent variables measured subsequent reading performance: recall, sentence completion and multiple choice. For recall, the researcher and an additional rater identified the total pausal units for the text. The interrater reliability index was .97. The total number of pausal units for the short story was 77, and for the essay the total number was 68. Separately the raters identified all possible correct responses for sentence completion items, and the interrater reliability index was .96. For multiple choice, there were four choices with one correct answer for each question.

For each research question, means, standard deviations, ranges, and median scores were calculated. To assess the degree to which the categorized items on the MARSI predicted reading scores on reading performance, data were examined using regression analysis. The regression procedure determined the strength of these relationships as well as the amount of variance explained by the categories of metacognition (Brantmeier, 2006a). The Alpha level for statistical significance was set at .05. In addition, data were analyzed to see which items of the three independent factors (global strategies, problem-solving strategies, and support strategies) had the highest bivariate correlation with comprehension when only significant independent predictors are entered into the regression equation. A regression model was calculated to determine which combination of significant predictors correlated with comprehension.

Results

Table 4.2 lists the mean scores and standard deviations for all three assessment tasks for both texts. The mean scores for all three assessment tasks were higher for the short story than the essay. With the recall task, participants only recalled approximately 9 units for the short story (possible score of 77) and 6 units for the essay (possible score of 68). It is interesting to note the wide range of scores for recall with both texts. For both texts some

TABLE 4.2   Mean Scores and Standard Deviations for Comprehension of Two Texts

	Recall		SC		MC	
	Txt1	Txt2	Txt1	Txt2	Txt1	Txt2
Possible score	77	68	10	10	10	10
Mean	8.7	6.1	4.8	2.3	8.0	3.5
SD	5.2	4.9	1.7	1.4	1.5	1.0
Minimum	2	3	0	0	4	0
Maximum	27	27	9	5	10	5
Range	25	25	9	5	6	5

Note: n = 129; Txt 1 = Short Story; Txt 2 = Essay

students recalled a maximum of 27 units, which is significantly higher than the average. Overall, however, recall scores are quite low considering that the group of readers is enrolled in an advanced Spanish grammar and composition course. With the sentence completion assessment task, students averaged 5 out of 10 for the short story and 2 out of 10 for the essay. With multiple-choice items readers scored 8 out of 10 for the short story and 4 out of 10 for the essay. Overall, in a comparison of comprehension scores for the short story and essay, readers achieved the highest scores on sentence completion and multiple choice items for the short story.

In order to examine whether the MARSI items yielded positive associations with reading performance, the three independent factors (global reading strategies, problem-solving reading strategies, and support reading strategies) were regressed on recall, sentence-completion and multiple-choice for the two different reading texts (short story and essay). With Text 1 (short story) and Text 2 (expository writing), 12 different items for global reading strategies were regressed on all three tasks (question #17 was omitted because it was not relevant to the story). Results yielded no positive association between overall global reading strategies and comprehension for Text 1 and Text 2. Eight different items for problem-solving strategies were regressed on all three tasks. Results yielded no positive association between overall problem-solving reading strategies and comprehension for Text 1 and Text 2. Finally, 8 different items for support reading strategies were regressed on all three tasks. Results yielded no positive association between overall support reading strategies and comprehension for Text 1 and Text 2.

Given the lack of significant findings for overall categories of items on the MARSI inventory, additional regression analysis were calculated in order to examine whether combinations of MARSI items by category were positively associated with subsequent reading performance. Results are listed on Tables 4.3 and 4.4 and detailed below.

Results: MARSI Items with Short Story

With the short story, several combinations of items from the global reading strategies category positively associated with performance on both sentence completion and multiple choice, but no combinations of items from the global reading strategies category were positively associated with performance on the written recall task. As indicated, global reading strategy Item #19 "I use context clues to help me better understand what I am reading" appeared in all combinations of significant associations for both sentence completion and multiple choice. For sentence completion, 4 different combinations of items provided positive associations. The combination of Item #19 with Item #23 "I critically analyze and evaluate the information presented in the text" appeared in most combinations of items that yielded positive

TABLE 4.3 Significant Associations between Combinations of MARSI Items by Category and All Comprehension Tasks for Short Story

Predictors (constant)	R^2	T-ratio	p
Global Reading Strategies			
Sentence-completion			
Item # 19	.04	4.5	.02*
Items # 19,23	.06	3.5	.01*
Items # 19,22,23	.07	3.6	.03*
Items# 14,19,22,23	.08	3.01	.04*
Multiple-choice			
Item # 19	.08	10.1	.00*
Items # 4,19	.10	9.7	.00*
Items # 1,4,19	.11	8.2	.00*
Items # 1,4,19,26	.12	8.3	.00*
Items # 1,3,4,19,26	.13	8.0	.01*
Items # 1,3,4,10,19,26	.13	8.0	.01*
Items # 1,3,4,10,14,19,26	.13	7.7	.02*
Items # 1,3,4,10,14,19,25,26	.13	7.4	.03*
Items # 1,3,4,10,14,19,22,25,26	.13	7.3	.04*
Problem-solving Reading Strategies			
Recall			
Items # 16,21,30	.13	0.6	.00*
Items # 11,16,21,30	.14	0.3	.00*
Items# 11,13,16,21,30	.15	0.6	.00*
Items # 11,13,16,21,27,30	.16	.41	.00*
Items # 8,11,13,16,21,27,30	.16	.44	.01*
Items# 8,11,13,16,18,21,27,30	.16	.44	.01*
Support Reading Strategies			
Recall			
Items # 2,24,28	.14	4.5	.00*
Items # 2,6,24,28	.15	3.4	.00*
Items # 2,6,20,24,28	.17	3.6	.00*
Items # 2,6,15,20,24,28	.18	2.3	.00*
Items # 2,6,12,15,20,24,28	.19	2.5	.00*
Items # 2,5,6,12,15,20,24,28	.20	2.3	.00*
Items # 2,5,6,9,12,15,20,24,28	.20	2.3	.00*
Multiple-choice			
Items # 5	.04	25.0	.02*
Items # 5,15	.06	13.0	.02*
Items # 5,15,20	.07	11.0	.04*

* $p < 0.05$; $n = 129$

TABLE 4.4 Significant Associations between Combinations of MARSI Items by Category and All Comprehension Tasks for Essay

Predictors (constant)	R^2	T-ratio	p
Global Reading Strategies			
Sentence-completion			
Items # 10,23,26	.10	2.4	.00*
Items # 10,23,26,29	.11	2.5	.01*
Items # 10,14,23,26,29	.12	1.8	.01*
Items # 4,10,14,23,26,29	.13	2.0	.01*
Items # 4,10,14,19,23,26,29	.14	2.3	.01*
Items # 4,10,14,19,23,25,26,29	.15	1.9	.01*
Items # 1,4,10,14,19,23,25,26,29	.16	2.1	.02*
Items # 1,4,7,10,14,19,23,25,26,29	.16	2.2	.03*
Items # 1,3,4,7,10,14,19,23,25,26,29	.16	2.1	.04*
Problem-solving Reading Strategies			
Recall			
Items # 21,30	.10	0.1	.00*
Items # 18,21,30	.11	0.1	.00*
Items # 11,18,21,30	.11	0.1	.01*
Items # 8,11,18,21,30	.12	0.2	.01*
Items # 8,11,16,18,21,30	.12	0.3	.03*
Items # 8,11,16,18,21,27,30	.12	1.1	.04*
Multiple-choice			
Item 21	.04	12.4	.03*
Support Reading Strategies			
Recall			
Items # 15,24,28	.10	2.1	.01*
Items # 12,15,24,28	.11	2.4	.01*
Items # 2,12,15,24,28	.12	2.2	.01*
Items # 2,6,12,15,24,28	.12	1.9	.02*
Items # 2,5,6,12,15,24,28	.12	1.9	.03*
Items# 2,5,6,12,15,20,24,28	.13	2.0	.04*
Sentence-completion			
Items # 12,15	.07	5.1	.01*
Items # 6,12,15	.09	4.0	.01*
Items # 6,12,15,24	.09	3.6	.03*
Multiple-choice			
Items # 6,12	.07	10.8	.03*
Items # 2,6,12	.07	11.2	.02*

* $p < 0.05$; $n = 129$

associations to scores on sentence-completion. Item #23 did not appear in any combinations of positive associations with multiple choice. For multiple choice, 9 different combinations of items yielded positive associations with Item #19 and Item #4 "I preview the text to see what it is about before reading it" holding the highest correlation.

Six combinations of items from the problem-solving category predict performance on recall, with the following three items holding the highest correlation: Item 16 "When text becomes difficult, I pay closer attention to what I am reading," Item #30 "I try to guess the meanings of unknown words or phrases," and Item #21 "I try to picture or visualize information to help remember what I read." No combinations of items from the problem-solving category predict performance on multiple choice or sentence completion for the short story.

Several combinations of items from the support reading strategies category predict performance on written recall and multiple choice, with a combination of three items yielding the highest correlation: Item #2 "I take notes while reading to help me understand what I read," Item #24 "I go back and forth in the text to find relationships among ideas in it" and Item #28 "I ask myself questions I like to have answered in the text." No combination of items from the support reading strategies positively associated with scores on sentence completion. For multiple choice Item #5 "When text becomes difficult, I read aloud to help me understand what I read" provided the highest correlation and appeared in all three combinations. The varied findings of combinations of metacognitive strategies with different assessment tasks for the short story lead to detailed explanation in the discussion section.

Results: MARSI Items with Essay

For the essay, assorted combinations of metacognitive strategies by category significantly predicted scores on different assessment tasks. Results are listed on Table 4.4. As indicated, no combinations of global reading strategies positively associated with recall or multiple choice for the essay. The following items yielded the highest correlation with sentence completion and appeared in all 9 combinations of positive associations with sentence completion: Item #10 "I skim the text first by noting characteristics like length and organization," Item #23 "I critically analyze and evaluate the information presented in the text," and #26 "I try to guess what the material is about that I read."

For problem-solving reading strategies, Item #21 "I try to picture or visualize information to help remember what I read" along with Item #30 "I try to guess the meaning of unknown words or phrases" provided the highest correlation with recall and appeared in all 6 combinations of items positively associated with recall. No positive associations were found for specific items from the problem solving reading strategies and sentence completion. The only Item that yielded a positive association with multiple choice was Item #21 "I try to picture or visualize information to help remember what I read."

For support reading strategies, 6 different combinations of items provided positive associations with recall. The following three items appeared in all combinations of positive associations with recall: Item # 15 "I use reference materials such as dictionaries to help me understand what I read," Item #24 "I go back and forth in the text to find relationships among ideas in it," and Item #28 "I ask myself questions I like to have answered in the text." Three different combinations of items yielded positive associations for sentence completion with Item #12 "I underline or circle information in the text to help me remember it" and Item #15 appearing in all combinations. Two different combinations of items provided a positive association with multiple choice, with Item #6 "I summarize what I read to reflect on important information in the text" and Item #12 "I underline and circle information in the text to help me remember it" appearing in both combinations. Again, the mixed results require thorough discussion.

DISCUSSION AND IMPLICATIONS

With regard to comprehension, the findings of the present study are similar to early investigations (Brantmeier, 2006a,b; Brantmeier & Vanderplank, 2008) where participants from advanced language courses scored low on L2 reading comprehension tasks, namely recall. For both the short story and the essay participants recalled approximately 9% of the total possible pausal units. This is very low for learners who placed into advanced level grammar and composition. Furthermore, when analyzing scores for sentence completion and multiple choice by text type, participants performed better on both sentence completion and multiple choice for the short story than for the essay. Students scored low on both sentence completion (2%) and multiple choice (4%) for the essay. A detailed discussion follows.

The online placement exam, completed by all participants prior to enrolling in the advanced course, tests vocabulary, grammar, listening and reading. Therefore, this exam may place weak readers into higher levels of language instruction because test takers may achieve high marks on listening and grammar. This may balance out low scores on reading as the total composite score determines placement. Results of the present study provide further evidence that readers placing into higher levels of language instruction may not have the skills necessary to process texts of higher difficulty levels. This, along with the fact that metacognitive deficits appear to be associated with comprehension difficulties, underscores the need for an effective inventory concerning metacognitive strategies. This inventory could be utilized by instructors in different ways to help students become more strategic readers.

Overall, the use of the MARSI, a metacognitive questionnaire composed of 3 different categories, allows practitioners to examine distinctive metacognitive strategies used during the L2 reading process. The findings in the present study indicate that the MARSI is an effective and informative inventory for use with adult L2 readers. More specifically, the MARSI consists of combinations of items that may predict achievement on different assessment tasks with different types of readings. As indicated above, across several studies with adult learners of Spanish enrolled in courses on advanced grammar and composition, findings revealed low scores on the written recall task. This merits a close examination of specific strategies that hold a positive association with recall. In the present study, with both the short story and essay a combination of two items from the problem-solving strategies provided positive associations with recall: Item #21 "I try to picture and visualize information to help remember what I read" and Item #30 "I try to guess the meaning of unknown words or phrases." These findings partially echo results from Padrón and Waxman (1988) where higher achieving ESL students imagined or pictured the story while reading. Given these results, instructors may want to dedicate class time to explaining and modeling these two effective problem-solving strategies. Instructors can read the text out loud to students and ask them to collectively take a moment to picture or visualize information to help comprehend and remember the text. Instructors may also want to demonstrate how to guess the meanings of unknown lexical items by utilizing contextual clues in the texts.

Additionally, with both the short story and essay the following combination of items from the support reading strategies yielded a positive association with recall: Item #24 "I go back and forth in the text to find relationships among ideas in it" and "I ask my self questions I like to have answered in the text." Both of these strategies require students to make predictions of text content. The process of making predictions, reading a segment of the text, and then pausing to confirm or reject comprehension can be effectively modeled by L2 instructors during class time. With sentence completion, only one item emerges with a positive association for both texts and this item is from the global reading strategy list: Item #23 "I critically analyze and evaluate the information presented in the text." No items appear to hold positive associations for multiple choice with both texts.

To turn to specific text types, with the short story, two different global reading strategies held positive associations with both sentence completion and multiple choice. Item #19 "I use context clues to help me better understand what I am reading" and Item # 14 "I decide what to read closely and what to ignore" appear in several combinations of items for both sentence completion and multiple choice. With the short story, only two items appeared in several combinations of items that yielded positive associations with multiple choice. Item #5 "When text becomes difficult, I read aloud to help me understand what I read" and Item #15 "I use reference materials such as dictionaries to help me understand what I read." Given the above combinations of strategies, instructors may want to ask students what they do when they encounter an unknown word while reading. The instructor can then direct a discussion that focuses on the availability and use of the above strategies. Additionally, instructors could develop a cloze instrument that consists of a reading with critical words omitted. With this instrument, students fill in the missing words while relying on the context to determine correct lexical items. Instructors can model how to use context clues to determine meanings of unknown words.

With the essay, three different global reading strategies appeared to have positive associations with sentence completion scores: Item #10 "I skim the text first by noting characteristics like length and organization," Item #23 "I critically analyze and evaluate the information presented in the text," and Item #26 "I try to guess what the material is about when I read." With the essay, one support reading strategy appears in combinations that provide positive associations with sentence completion and multiple choice: Item #12 "I underline or circle information in the text to help me remember it." As McKeown and Gentilucci (2007) point out, the efficiency of reading strategies depends on the needs of students across different levels of language instruction. The present study reveals that the above combination of global reading strategies are useful for learners at the advanced stage of acquisition, and these strategies can be taught and modeled by instructors in the classroom in order to enhance comprehension. Various second language studies have shown significant positive effects for strategy training when compared to traditional approaches to instruction (Barnett, 1988; Jimenez, 1997; Kern, 1989). Specifically, Barnett's (1988) findings indicated that comprehension scores increased with the use of "reading through context" and also with increasing self-perception of effective strategy use.

Carrell and Carson (1993) found that L1 readers with high comprehension were also high L2 comprehenders, but they were careful to note that readers did not use the same strategies to read in both languages. Van Gelderen et al. (2004) conclude that metacognitive knowledge influences both L1 and L2 reading comprehension and that L1 reading accounts for a substantial portion of variance in L2 reading comprehension. In the present study, all students in the investigation were full time students at a private, Midwestern university with a very strict admission process that requires high scores on the verbal sections of the SAT and ACT. In the present experiment, the advanced learners did not achieve high comprehension scores as measured via recall, sentence completion, and multiple choice, and this substantiates the claim that L2 reading strategies need to be emphasized in the classroom. Consequently, it may be said that the learners are good L1 readers, but poor L2 readers. Before any assertion can be drawn, a future study should include a test of L1 reading within the methodology and design of the present study.

The strategies noted above can be demonstrated and practiced collectively in the classroom. Traditionally, reading is seen as an individual act with reading assignments completed silently at home before coming to class. The results of the present study call for reading to be viewed as a social act in the advanced levels of language instruction so that students can learn from both the instructor and their peers. The approach of involving students in the process of reading is not new (Auerbach & Paxton, 1997). These researchers use think-aloud protocols to help students examine their first and second language reading strategies, and they specifically discuss how think-alouds can help develop metacognitive strategies. Carrell et al. (1989) findings further substantiate the need to train and teach metacognitive strategies in the classroom. Through collective attention given to strategies in the classroom, individual students will learn from each other and will also be able to self-diagnose strengths and weaknesses in the reading process.

CONCLUSION

Overall, the present study revealed that the MARSI can be used with adult, advanced L2 learners to assess the use of metacognitive strategies and their associations with comprehension. Specifically, certain combinations of items revealed positive associations for different texts and types of assessment tasks with advanced language learners. Consequently, instructors may want to consider combinations of results when teaching metacognitive strategies in the classroom, and the MARSI may aid instructors to diagnose strengths and weaknesses of individual readers. As Anderson (2003) boldly states, the instruction of L2 metacognitive reading skills may be the most valuable use of instructional time. Given the low reading comprehension scores with advanced learners cited in this chapter, instructors need to incorporate strategy training as part of the L2 classroom experience. Direct strategy instruction and modeling must be made available for readers so that they can determine their unique needs at the advanced levels of language instruction.

REFERENCES

Anderson, N. (2003). Metacognitive reading strategies increase L2 performance. *The Language Teacher, 27*(7), 20–22.

Auerbach, E. R., & Paxton, D. (1997). "It's not the English thing:" Bringing reading research into the ESL classroom. *TESOL Quarterly, 31*, 237–261.

Baker, L., & Brown, A. L. (1984). Metacognitive skills in reading. In P.D. Pearson, M. Kamil, R. Barr, & P. Mosenthal (Eds.), *Handbook of reading research* (Vol. 1, pp. 353–394). New York: Longman.

Bell, J. (2007). Indian and Bangladeshi perspectives: Use of metacognition and framing in postgraduate study. *Language Awareness, 16*(2), 81–98.

Barnett, M. A. (1988). Reading through context: How real and perceived strategy use affects L2 comprehension. *Modern Language Journal, 72*, 150–160.

Bernhardt, E. B. (2005). Progress and procrastination in second language reading. *Annual Review of Applied Linguistics, 25*, 133–150.

Bernhardt, E. B. & Kamil, M. L. (1995). Interpreting relationships between L1 and L2 reading: Consolidating the linguistic threshold and the linguistic interdependence hypotheses. *Applied Linguistics, 16*(2), 16–34.

Bossers, B. (1991). On thresholds, ceiling, and short circuits: The relation between L1 reading, L2 reading and L1 knowledge. *AILA Review, 8*, 45–60.

Brantmeier, C. (2005). Nonlinguistic variables in advanced second language reading: Learners' self-assessment and enjoyment. *Foreign Language Annals, 38*(4), 494–504.

Brantmeier, C. (2006a). Toward a multicomponent model of interest and second language reading: Sources of interest, perceived situational interest, and comprehension. *Reading in a Foreign Language, 18*(2), 89–115.

Brantmeier, C. (2006b). Advanced L2 learners and reading placement: Self-assessment, computer-based testing, and subsequent performance. *System, 34*(1), 15–35.

Brantmeier, C., & Vanderplank, R. (2008). Descriptive and criterion-referenced self-assessment with L2 readers. *System, 36*, 456–477.

Brisbois, J. (1995). Connections between first- and second language reading. *Journal of Reading Behavior, 24*, 565–584.

Brown, A. (1987a). Metacognition, executive control, self-regulated and other more mysterious mechanisms. In F. Weinert & R. Kluwe (Eds.), *Metacognition, motivation, and understanding* (pp. 65–116). Hillsdale, NJ: Lawrence Erlbaum Associates.

Brown, A. L. (1987b). Knowing when, where, and how to remember: A problem of metacognition. *Advances in Instructional Psychology, 1*, 77–165.

Carrell, P. L. (1991). Second language reading: Reading ability or language proficiency? *Applied Linguistics, 12*, 159–179.

Carrell, P. L. (1989). Metacognitive awareness and second language reading. *Modern Language Journal. 73*(2), 121–134.

Carrell, P. L., & Carson, J. G. (1993). First and second language reading strategies: Evidence from cloze. *Reading in a Foreign Language, 10*(1), 953–965.

Carrell, P. L., Pharis, B. G., & Liberto, J.C. (1989). Metacognitive strategy training for ESL reading. *TESOL Quarterly. 23*(4), 647–678.

Devine, J. (1993). The role of metacognition in second language reading and writing. In J.G. Carson & I. Leki (Eds.),Reading in the composition classroom: Second language perspectives (pp. 105–127). Boston: Heinle & Heinle.

Dickinson, L. (1995). Autonomy and motivation: A literature review. *System, 23*(2), 165–174.

Fajar, L., Santos, K., & Tobias, S. (1996). *Knowledge monitoring among bilingual students.* Paper presented at the annual meeting of the Northeastern Educational Research Association, Ellenville, NY.

Fotovatian, S., & Shokrpour, N. (2007). Comparison of the efficiency of reading comprehension strategies on Iranian university students' comprehension. *Journal of College Reading and Learning, 37*(2), 47–63.

Goodman, K. S. (1971). Psycholinguistic universals in the reading process. In P. Pimsleur & T. Quinn (Eds.), *The psychology of second language reading* (pp. 135–142). Cambridge: Cambridge University Press.

Jiménez, R. T. (1997). The strategic reading abilities and potential of five low-literacy Latina/o readers in middle school. *Reading Research Quarterly, 32*(3), 224–243.

Kern, R. G. (1989). Second language reading strategy instruction: Its effects on comprehension and word inference ability. *Modern Language Journal, 73,* 135–149.

Kolić-Vehovec, S., & Bajšanski, I. (2007). Comprehension monitoring and reading comprehension in bilingual students. *Journal of Research in Reading, 30*(2), 198–211.

Layton, A., Robinson, J., & Lawson, M. (1998, February). The relationship between syntactic awareness and reading performance. *Journal of Research in Reading, 21*(1), 5–23.

Lee, J. F. (1986). On the use of the recall task to measure L2 reading comprehension. *Studies in Second Language Acquisition, 8,* 201–212.

McKeown, R. G., & Gentilucci, J. L. (2007). Think-aloud strategy: Metacognitive development and monitoring comprehension in the middle school second-language classroom. *Journal of Adolescent & Adult Literacy, 51*(2), 136–147.

Mokhtari, K., & Reichard, C. A. (2002). Assessing students' metacognitive awareness of reading strategies. *Journal of Educational Psychology, 94*(2), 249–259.

O'Malley, J. M., & Chamot, A. U. (1990). *Learning strategies in second language acquisition.* Cambridge: Cambridge University Press.

Owings, R. A., & Petersen, G. A. (1980). Spontaneous monitoring and regulation of learning: A comparison of successful and less successful fifth graders. *Journal of Educational Psychology, 72*(2), 252–256.

Padrón, Y. N., & Waxman, H. C. (1988). The effect of ESL students' perceptions of their cognitive reading strategies on reading achievement. *TESOL Quarterly, 22*(1), 146–150.

Romero, R., & Tobias, S. (1996). *Knowledge monitoring and strategic study.* Paper presented at a symposium on "Metacognitive Knowledge Monitoring" at the annual convention of the Northeaster Educational Research Association, Ellenville, NY.

Shohamy, E. (1982). Affective considerations in language testing. *Modern Language Journal, 66,* 13–17.

Shohamy, E. (1984). Does the testing method make the difference? The case of reading comprehension. *Language Testing, 1,* 147–170.

Tobias, S., & Everson, H. (2002). *Knowing what you know and what you don't: Further research on metacognitive knowledge monitoring.* College Board Report No. 2002–3. College Board, NY.

Tobias, S., Everson, H. T., Laitusis, V., & Fields, M. (1999, April). *Metacognitive knowledge monitoring: Domain specific or general?* Paper presented at the annual meeting of the Society for the Scientific Study of Reading, Montreal.

Van Gelderen, A., Schoonen, R., de Glopper, K., Hulstijn, J., Snellings, P., Simis, A., & Stevenson, M. (2003). Roles of linguistic knowledge, metacognitive knowledge, and processing speed in L3, L2, and L1 reading comprehension: A structural equation modeling approach. *International Journal of Bilingualism.* 7(1), 7–25.

Van Gelderen, A., Schoonen, R., de Glopper, K., Hulstijn, J., Simis, A., Snellings, P., & Stevenson, M. (2004). Linguistic knowledge, processing speed, and metacognitive knowledge in first- and second-language reading comprehension: A componential analysis. *Journal of Educational Psychology, 96*(1), 19–30.

Verhoeven, L. T. (1990). Acquisition of reading in a second language. *Reading Research Quarterly, 25*(2), 90–114.

Wolf, D. (1993). A comparison of assessment tasks used to measure FL reading comprehension. *Modern Language Journal, 77,* 473–489.

Zimmerman, B. J., & Bandura, A. (1994). Impact of self-regulatory influences on writing course attainment. *American Educational Research Journal, 31*(4), 845–862.

Zimmerman, B. J. (1989). Models of self-regulated learning and academic achievement. In B. J. Zimmerman & D. H. Schunk (Eds.), *Self-regulated learning and academic achievement: Theory, research, and practice* (pp. 1–25). New York: Springer-Verlag.

APPENDIX
List of Categories of Items on MARSI Inventory

Item # On Inventory and Corresponding Item:

Global Reading Strategies
1. I have a purpose in mind when I read.
3. I think about what I know to help me understand what I read.
4. I preview the text to see what it's about before reading it.
7. I think about whether the content of the text fits my reading purpose.
10. I skim the text first by noting characteristics like length and organization.
14. I decide what to read closely and what to ignore.
17. I use tables, figures, and pictures in text to increase my understanding.
19. I use context clues to help me better understand what I'm reading.
22. I use typographical aids like boldface and italics to identify key information.
23. I critically analyze and evaluate the information presented in the text.
25. I check my understanding when I come across conflicting information.
26. I try to guess what the material is about when I read.
29. I check to see if my guesses about the text are right or wrong.

Problem-Solving Strategies
8. I read slowly but carefully to be sure I understand what I'm reading.
11. I try to get back on track when I lose concentration.
13. I adjust my reading speed according to what I'm reading.
16. When text becomes difficult, I pay closer attention to what I'm reading.
18. I stop from time to time and think about what I'm reading.
21. I try to picture or visualize information to help remember what I read.
27. When text becomes difficult, I reread to increase my understanding.
30. I try to guess the meaning of unknown words or phrases.

Support Reading Strategies
2. I take notes while reading to help me understand what I read.
5. When text becomes difficult, I read aloud to help me understand what I read.
6. I summarize what I read to reflect on important information in the text.
12. I underline or circle information in the text to help me remember it.
15. I use reference materials such as dictionaries to help me understand what I read.
20. I paraphrase (restate ideas in my own words) to better understand what I read.
24. I go back and forth in the text to find relationships among ideas in it.
28. I ask myself questions I like to have answered in the text.

CHAPTER 5

WHAT DON'T YOU UNDERSTAND?

Understanding Misunderstandings in Foreign Language Reading

Dolly J. Young and Constancio K. Nakuma

ABSTRACT

In spoken Foreign Language (FL) discourse, some misunderstandings can actually lead to further negotiation of meaning, and ultimately clarification. What happens, however, when misunderstandings occur in the context of FL reading? The parameters of negotiability become more limited, although negotiation of sorts occurs. Research on misunderstandings in discourse written in a FL is sparse, albeit such research could further our knowledge of the reading process and inform interactive models of FL reading. In the research we report here, we analyze 120 reading recalls of a Spanish passage that obtained a significantly higher number of misunderstandings compared to three other passages to ascertain what was misunderstood and why. Our subjects were second-year Spanish students enrolled in an intensive six-hours-per-day three-week program at a large state university. Our analysis of the reading recalls, which were written in English, indicated that most misunder-

Crossing Languages and Research Methods, pages 73–95

standings fell into two broad categories: linguistically-based and cognitively-related misunderstandings. These conspired to break down comprehension. As a result of our analysis, we profile the reading behavior of FL learners of limited FL proficiency when faced with a culturally laced topic of which they have little knowledge. Our findings suggest that readers process the language they understand and then, because of propositional deficits and limited language proficiency, they fill in the gaps with propositions that work at that particular juncture, irrespective of whether they make sense or follow any cohesive thread.

INTRODUCTION

Misunderstandings, miscommunications, communicative breakdowns, mix-ups, confusions, misinterpretations are all common phenomena within members of the same speech community. The severity of a misunderstanding can range from mild to catastrophic. Consequently, researchers from a range of disciplines, from the social sciences to the humanities, have harvested a substantial body of research on misunderstandings. That corpus of research has helped to (a) explain sources that lead to misconstructions and to variables that influence misunderstandings, (b) provide taxonomies that describe types of misunderstandings, (c) examine approaches to analyzing misunderstandings in spoken discourse, (d) identify consequences of misinterpretations, and (e) analyze cross-cultural misunderstandings (see House, Kasper, & Ross, 2003).

Given the large number of studies from various disciplines and the numerous approaches to this topic, imagine the variety, number, and analytical approaches potentially generated from misunderstandings that occur when confronted with a foreign language and a culture distinct from your own, as is the case for the foreign language learner. Interestingly, in SPOKEN foreign-language (FL) discourse some misunderstandings can actually lead to further negotiation of meaning and ultimately clarification. What happens, however, when misunderstandings occur in the context of FL READING? The parameters of negotiability become more limited, although negotiation of sorts occurs. Research on misunderstandings in discourse written in a FL is sparse, albeit such research could further our knowledge of this phenomenon and inform current interactive models of FL reading.

The study reported here evolved from a previous study on the effects of textual simplification on FL reading comprehension (Young, 1999) when one of four expository texts given to second-year Spanish students resulted in a significantly higher number of misunderstandings. In other words, students read four different articles and only one, entitled "La Virgen de Guadalupe es un 'misterio no resuelto,'" resulted in significantly more misunderstandings compared to the other three (see Appendix A for the Spanish version and appendix B for an English translation of this text). For the present research, we aspired to identify the factors that led to the increased number of misunderstandings and to investigate whether there were common misunderstandings that were shared by learners, and how meaning was negotiated when misunderstandings did surface.

FL READING RESEARCH

In the last thirty years, research in FL reading has consistently indicated that multiple factors influence comprehension of written discourse. To achieve successful reading comprehension, a form of negotiation of meaning occurs, much like in spoken discourse, based on a range of variables related to the reader and the text. With regard to the reader, those variables are based on experience, how much knowledge is brought to the text by the reader in terms of familiarity with the topic (Anderson & Pearson, 1984; Carrell 1983a,b, 1987) and with rhetorical structures (Carrell 1984, 1992; Hague & Scott 1994), native language ability and foreign language proficiency (Anderson & Pearson, 1984; Bernhardt, 1984; Bernhardt & Kamil, 1995; Lee & Schallert, 1997). A logical conclusion to this body of research suggests that background knowledge, in its various manifestations (see Alexander, Schallert, & Hare 1991) and FL proficiency can help to reduce misunderstandings. Moreover, the research indicates that text-related variables that must be taken into account for successful reading comprehension to occur include the length of the text (Leow, 1997b), the sentence complexity (Blau, 1982; Hoover, 1992), the degree of textual/discourse coherence, and the text voice (Beck, McKeown, & Worthy, 1995). Enveloping the reader and the text is a social reality. In addition to considerations of the reader and the text, cross-cultural miscommunications can surface as a result of differences at an ideological level (Kramsch, 2003). Kramsch's research illustrates how "the institutions that regulate people's lives as organizations of power and control are believed to impose their ideology on the discourse of individual speakers..." (p. 129) and can thus result in misunderstandings and misinterpretations.

Most of the research in FL reading attempts to explore variables that enhance or impede reading comprehension in a FL, from Ll-reading and FL proficiency to reading strategies. L2 proficiency is of chief importance to understanding FL discourse; consequently, researchers have investigated various linguistic aspects of FL reading, such as whether linguistic complexity cancels the advantage of topic familiarity in a reading or vice versa (Barry & Lazarte, 1995; Johnson, 1981; Lee & Schallert, 1997). The cornucopia of FL reading research has served to develop potential theories and models of FL reading, which in turn have advanced our understanding of the FL reading process and product. With the exception of a handful of articles, however, few have actually examined qualitatively the processes FL learners use to negotiate meaning from a FL text (Maxim, 2000). Instead, most researchers use quantitative methods of analysis, i.e., reading comprehension scores, as the dependent variable and reader or text variables as independent variables to discuss successful or unsuccessful reading comprehension.

Armed with 120 recalls from second-year Spanish students and a text that had a high level of misunderstandings, we sought to investigate what FL learners misunderstood, why and what happened to the reading process as a result.

METHOD

Background

In Young (1999), as we scored the recalls of four different texts, we became increasingly aware of the inconsistencies between some recall scores (using weighted pausal units)[1] and an actual comprehensive and cohesive understanding of the passage. Some students obtained decent scores on the recalls, but those scores did not seem to indicate an integration of ideas or events. Moreover, some students ended up with relatively good recall scores, yet important misunderstandings occurred. Consequently, we created three separate criteria for re-scoring the recalls. We scored them by Main Idea, Created Discourse (offering supporting arguments, examples or details from the text), and Misunderstandings[2] (see Young, 1999, for results). Of the four texts we used in the 1999 study (see Table 5.1 for characteristics of the initial four texts), only "La Virgen de Guadalupe es un 'misterio no resuelto'" achieved a particularly high score on misunderstandings. It proved to be significantly different ($F = 14.6$, $p > .0001$) in the number of misunderstandings from the other three texts.

We also administered a separate questionnaire to students to address their familiarity with the text topics. We asked students to indicate, using a Likert scale from 5 CI (was very knowledgeable about the topic of this reading) to 1 CI (knew absolutely nothing about the topic in this reading), how familiar they were with the topic of each text. We found, however, no significant relationship between students' familiarity with the topics of the four texts and their recall scores. For the text "La Virgen de Guadalupe es un 'misterio no resuelto,'" we suspect that students' familiarity with NBC and the TV series called "Unsolved Mysteries" may have led them to perceive that as the topic of this text, instead of the actual mystery/miracle. We arrived at this conclusion only after scoring the recalls, because in them

TABLE 5.1 Characteristics of Four Spanish Texts Used in the Original Study (Young 1999)

Text title	Structure	FRASE[a]	Words
A 'El Portuñol' [*Magazine article*]	Causation text structure	Advanced intermediate (Level III)	456
B "La Virgen de Guadalupe ..." [*Newspaper article*]	collection text structure	Intermediate (Level II)	412
C 'Traductores sin licencia' [*Magazine article*]	problem/solution text structure	Intermediate (Level II)	646
D 'El apóstol de los indígenas ...' [*Magazine article*]	collection text structure	Advanced intermediate (Level III)	581

[a] FRASE = Fry Adaptation for Spanish Evaluation (Vari-Cartier 1981)

students repeatedly cited the program "Unsolved Mysteries" in some form or fashion, indicating a familiarity with this TV program, and because students' recalls did not convey much information regarding the actual mystery, the miracle.

All 127 students read all four texts. Considering that their language proficiency was the same across texts, we could not attribute misunderstandings to readability levels, since students appeared to understand more from texts with readability levels higher than this one, and that only this one seemed to trigger many more misunderstandings than the others, we sought to investigate the variables that could explain the high number of misunderstandings this text produced.

The variables that differentiate "La Virgen de Guadalupe es un 'misterio no resuelto'" from the others include: (a) a substantial portion of this text dealt with a cultural phenomenon for which students had no cultural reference,[3] even though they may have been familiar with the TV show "Unsolved Mysteries," (b) it was a newspaper article, while the other three were magazine articles, and (c) it was shorter that the other three texts but even then, was rated a lower readability level (Intermediate Level II) than two of the others, which were rated as Advanced.[4]

These three variables can be significant for successful FL reading comprehension, however. In general terms, newspaper articles do not provide the type of clues that have been shown to enhance reading comprehension, such as pictures, subtitles, headings, subheadings, but the fact is that this particular newspaper article did. It had all of those features. The length of a text can also affect reading comprehension (Leow, 1997b). This text was shorter than the other three, but only by 33 words and it was longer than the text used in Leow (1997b).[5] Nevertheless, newspaper articles and shorter texts may lack the textual voice and the cohesion that tend to improve FL reading comprehension (Beck et al., 1995). The other difference between this text and the other three rests with the text content, which was foreign to the students. According to Patricia Johnson (1981), when cultural knowledge is missing from the reader, the reader is "more dependent on the language of the text for interpretation" (p. 180).

Armed with this knowledge, we proceeded to investigate the kinds of misunderstandings that surfaced in the student recalls and to identify their potential sources.

Subjects

The subjects were second-year Spanish students—56 females and 71 males—enrolled in an intensive Spanish program that met six hours every day for three weeks. The program was offered every May at a large state land grant university. All students enrolled in that program participated in this study.

Procedures

We directed subjects to read all instructions before beginning and to take as much time as they needed because afterward they would be asked to recall as much as they could about the text, from general ideas to details. After reading the text, they turned it into the instructor and collected two sheets of paper, one yellow and one green. On the yellow paper, the students could jot down ideas, notes, or details to reduce memory limitations. On the green sheet of paper, they were to organize their notes to reflect what they comprehended from the text. Afterward, students turned in their notes and completed recalls and were given a multiple-choice reading comprehension test about the text, which included several open-ended questions.[6]

Analysis

We analyzed 120 student recalls (7 absences) of the text "La Virgen de Guadalupe es un 'misterio no resuelto'" (see Appendix A). In addition, we examined the multiple-choice and open-ended answers for further insights into the students' misunderstandings. We identified and classified the participants' responses on the open-ended comprehension test as well as the recall sheets, to sort through ambiguous statements. Misunderstandings were then identified, and patterns were documented based on the number of times they occurred. Once we had documented the actual misunderstandings, we turned our attention to what they had in common to arrive at types of misunderstandings. The types fell into two broad categories. After comparing our initial findings, we developed a preliminary list of rubrics and categories, which we ultimately fine-tuned, by contrasting the language of the text with what students had understood the text to mean. We examined the conceptual and language-related characteristics of the original text at the sentence, paragraph, and discourse level (where that was feasible) to arrive at some possible explanations for the misunderstandings. We also deduced sources of misunderstanding. This latter technique was used especially where information was added to the storyline by the subject and could not, therefore, be traced to any part of the text. In this next section, we present and discuss our results.

RESULTS

General Trends

We found discernable patterns in the misunderstandings registered by participants, which fell into two broad categories (see Table 5.2). The first type of misunderstanding consisted of the readers taking specific wording, sentences or entire paragraphs to mean something totally different from the intended meaning. We refer to these types of misunderstandings as LINGUISTICALLY BASED MISUNDERSTANDINGS and attribute students' interlanguage status to them. In other words, students' inadequate knowledge of the language code may explain those misunderstandings.

The second type of misunderstanding occurred at the conceptual level, and we refer to these as COGNITIVELY RELATED MISUNDERSTANDINGS because they were largely attributable to propositional deficits. More specifically, those misunderstandings consisted of the participants' compensating for perceived logical gaps in the storyline by simply rewriting the text to fit their assumptions. The compensatory behavior was initiated by students' deficiencies in their linguistic skills and content familiarity and led to propositional deficits in the storyline of the text.

These two categories are not necessarily separate or independent, since they appear to work together in the reading process to explain the misunderstandings that surfaced in this particular text. While these general tendencies are interesting in that they provide some insight into how participants processed the text during reading, the details of what was actually recalled are even more revealing of the psycholinguistic-dynamics of reading comprehension.

TABLE 5.2 Categories of Misunderstandings

Linguistically based misunderstandings attributable to:

Phrase structure length and complexity
    Long and complex sentences
    Subject–verb inversion and distance
    Number of embedded clauses in the sentence

Lexical variables
    Unfamiliar vocabulary
    False cognates
    Unfamiliar or unrecognized verb meanings

Morphological and grammatical variables
    Form-meaning connections
    Prepositions
    Conjunctions, connectors

Idiomatic expressions (relative clauses)

Cognitively related misunderstandings due to propositional deficits attributable to:

Reliance on extra-textual logic
Inability to confirm information
Lack of storyline connections
Lack of cultural schemata for organizing cultural concepts

Linguistically Based Misunderstandings

Paragraphs 1, 3, 5, and 7 accounted for the highest number of linguistically-based misunderstandings (see Appendix A). These particular paragraphs contained any combination of complex phrase structures, such as sentences with embedded clauses, subject-verb or verb-object inversions, phrase structure length, lexical and morphological variables, and/or phrases/expressions (relative clauses). The following features of the language in the text help explain the most common misunderstandings that surfaced in the students' recalls.

Phrase Structure Complexity

The following sentence in paragraph 5 of the text, characterized by subject-verb inversions and an embedded clause, was the source of numerous misunderstandings associated with the details of the storyline, nuances in the story, and event sequencing:

> La aparición pidió a Juan Diego que en ese Lugar sobre la falda del cerro del Tepeyac se construyera un templo en su honor, desde el cual ella extendería su protección al pueblo de México.

[The apparition asked Juan Diego that in that very place at the lower slope of the hills of Tepeyac a temple be constructed in her honor from which she would extend her protection over the town of Mexico.]

This complex sentence was misinterpreted in a wide variety of ways, including, but certainly not limited to, the following:

a. She told him to promote Christianity in Mexico.
b. He later then built a statue of the image which is supposed to protect Mexico.
c. A temple was built to house the painting in Cerro.
d. Juan Diego constructed a temple in her honor to extend his protection.

These examples suggest that students relied heavily on their native language syntax to decode a complex sentence. Where there was a subject-verb inversion, the subject was mistaken to be a direct object. For example, *apareció una pintura* (¶7) was rendered as "[Juan-Diego] painted a picture."

Lexical Factors

Often, unknown words led to important misunderstandings—such as not knowing that the word *capa* meant "cloak" or were entirely omitted, such as *mensaje, obispo, veracidad, agregado,* or *transcurso.*

Frequently, participants appeared to treat unfamiliar vocabulary words as proper nouns. For example, in several recalls, the word *cerro* was mistaken for the name of a place, just as *basilica* was rendered a place, as either *Bastilia* or *Basilica.* When it came to not knowing the meaning of a word, it was deleted from the storyline, or else participants became creative by attributing some type of meaning to the word and then making it fit at some point, regardless of how senseless or illogical it appeared. For example, the following excerpt illustrates how the participant took the word *habilidad* (¶11) to be some nonexistent technical term "habilitas":

> By the end of the segment NBC had some thoughts and ideas on this mysterious figure. One of the strongest things to understand about it all is it contained modern habilitas. This left everyone clueless.

Another interpretation is that "habilitas" was interpreted as "abilities" or "skills" because of its resemblance to the English word.

This leads to another common linguistically-based misunderstanding stemming from FL learners' over reliance on cognates. Cognates can be useful in reading comprehension, and recognizing them is a strategy that works well for the reader. For example, the subjunctive morphology, while probably unfamiliar to participants, did not interfere with processing the storyline if the stem was from a recognizable cognate, as in the word *construyera*. Most participants understood something was to be constructed. Some cognates, however, are false cognates and can interfere with the reading process. In many of the recalls there was a pattern of rendering look-alikes into cognates, whether they were authentic cognates or not, and as a result, leading to several important misunderstandings. The following are examples of such occurrences.

- *capa* (¶11 2) was rendered as "hat" and "cave"
- *Este segmento, que sera transmitido por la NBC esta temporada* (¶11) was misunderstood as "... The television show is only temporary."
- *gobiernos* (governments, ¶ 9) was rendered as "governors."
- *pidió una prueba* (¶5) was interpreted as "shared it with the people" (*prueba* might have been confused with *pueblo*, and *pidió* not understood).

The most significant misunderstanding stemmed from rendering *capa* as "cave" or "hat," particularly because the key element of the storyline revolved around Juan Diego's "cloak," *capa*.

Interestingly, while many students made the connection between *Misterios no resueltos* and the television series "Unsolved Mysteries," this phrase was commonly decoded in the following ways:

a. "mysteries without results," "mysteries and no results," "mysteries no results" "mysteries with no results," "mystery of missing men," "the mystery of all this";
b. "mysterious occurrences," "mysterious stories from history in Mexico";
c. title not provided.

Three patterns reveal the processes participants employed to negotiate meaning from this phrase. First, there is a pattern of literally fitting every cognate into the storyline, as illustrated in the examples in (a). Second, there is the pattern of forward processing from the identified cognate, as illustrated by examples in (b), whereby the storyline following the cognate is deduced on the basis of the identified cognate. In this case, when *misterios* is identified as an adjective equivalent to the English *mysterious*, the *resueltos* is treated as a noun and hence ignored for not making any sense if translated as "results." Other nouns in English that could possibly go with "mysterious" in the context of the story are then proposed (e.g., "stories," "occurrences"). Interestingly, no participant interpreted *misterios no resueltos* as "mysterious results" or "mysterious no results," although *misterios* is joined with "results" using a conjunction or preposition. The third pattern, illustrated by (c), is for the reader simply to treat the phrase as a chunk, and/or to provide the English title. This particular pattern might indicate a direct and clearer association with the NBC TV series and could be suggestive of better reading skills.

It is easy to see how the presence of false cognates in a text, such as *resueltos* (which looks like "results"), could increase the level of difficulty for FL readers, since they can point the reader away from the correct meaning. In this particular case, the interpretations in (a) and (b) could still convey a general notion of a mystery and of that mystery not being resolved, i.e., of not having results. That meaning, however, only makes sense because of students' familiarity with the TV series "Unsolved Mysteries." On the other hand, the word *capa*, as "cave" or "hat," broke down crucial elements needed to adequately process the text and its storyline.

Morphological and Grammatical Markers

Another source of misunderstandings surfaced from misinterpretation of, or inattentiveness to, tense or aspect and agreement clues. Either the subjunctive morphology was unknown to the participants, or the verb stems were not recognized in the following verbs, which were omitted by the majority of participants: *recogiera, pudiera*, and *pusiera.*

Reference to grammatical markers encompasses such word functions as prepositions and conjunctions. The direction of Juan-Diego's travel from Tlatelolco was reversed to "followed to Tlatelolco," when the preposition in *iba camino de la ciudad de Tlatelolco* (¶3) was misunderstood. The preposition *de* in... *al norte de la ciudad de Mexico* (¶3) was misunderstood as "Juan Diego, an Aztec missionary, was walking *in* a city near Mexico." The preposition *a* in *convertidos a la fe* (¶3) was understood to mean "Juan Diego was a missionary and converted the Aztecs"; "Juan Diego, a missionary to convert Aztecs"; "Juan Diego, the first Aztec"; and "Juan Diego, one of the first Spanish missionaries in the Post-Aztec era." The prepositional phrase *después de la de* in the phrase... *es la más popular del mundo católico después de la de San Pedro en el Vaticano* (¶10) was often misunderstood as "between," as in "[a]bout 10 million people come from anywhere between San Padre to the Vatican to catch a glimpse of the Virgin Mary."

Idiomatic Expressions and Relative Clauses

Most of the time these tend to be ignored. Without fail, the relative clauses *desde el cual, de la cual,* and *lo que* were particularly problematic and led to misunderstandings or omissions. The sentence *La aparición pidió a Juan Diego... se construyera un templo en su honor, desde el cual ella extendería su protección al pueblo de México* (¶5) was consistently misunderstood, or the information after the relative clause was entirely omitted, as in the following examples:

1. He had a temple built to protect the Virgin Mary from the Aztecs and people of Mexico;
2. Juan had a temple built to honor and worship the artifact as well as to protect it from invaders;
3. The apparition told Diego that the temple was going to be destroyed;
4. He decided he would build a temple for her.

What makes these linguistically-based misunderstandings significant is when it leads to a <u>general</u> misunderstanding of key elements in the storyline.

Cognitively Related Misunderstandings

In attempts to negotiate meaning with the text, portions of the storyline that were not picked up during the reading caused the overall storyline to be incoherent and made it necessary for the reader to supply propositions to restore that logic. For example, a complex sentence might be simplified to its keyword elements, which the reader then uses to construct propositions for the entire sentence. When participants encountered a difficult paragraph, their storyline got disrupted, causing them to skip to the next comprehensible segment of the story, and to bridge any inconsistencies by adding information not provided in the text.

There were two key paragraphs in the text that were entirely omitted in the majority of the student recalls. Paragraphs 6 and 7 were deleted in most of the recalls:

¶ 6: Juan Diego regresó al mismo lugar y fue instruido por la aparición para que recogiera todas las rosas que pudiera encontrar en el lugar, y que las pusiera dentro de su capa para llevarlas al obispo, los cual hizo.

[Juan Diego returned to the same place and was instructed by the apparition to collect all the roses that he could find around there and to put them in his cloak to take them to the bishop, all of which he did.]

¶ 7: Cuando Juan Diego abrió su capa frente al obispo, los pétalos de las rosas cayeron al suelo y apareció una pintura desconocida de la Virgen María.

[When Juan Diego unfolded his cloak in front of the bishop, the rose petals fell to the ground and an unfamiliar painting of the Virgin Mary appeared.]

The following recall illustrates how this particular participant, who had a good score on the recall, created his own understanding (or misunderstanding) of the text:

NBC is going to do a show on the Virgin Mary and her magnificent glow of light. This mystery was shown on NBC's Unsolved Mysteries because it was so big. Juan left his cave and went to town. While he was gone, a bright light was seen at his cave, and when he returned there was a beautiful painting of the Virgin Mary. He was with a lady friend one night when they saw the image of the Virgin Mary. He later then built a statue of the image which is supposed to protect Mexico. The statue has unique details and magnificent paintings. Juan Diego saw light radiating from a painting of the Virgin Mary. A temple was built to house the painting in Cerro. People brought roses and left them with the painting. Mary told him to paint a picture of her with rose petals and something else. Juan Diego went and told people and something happened to the petals of roses he brought. Images of Guadalupe is an exhibit of these paintings in the city of Basilica. Investigations went on for four years. For ten years, this was a big tourist attraction. Since his death, the Virgin Mary has been seen standing over his grave many times in the last 400 years. The Virgin Mary seems to come to life with bright colors and brilliant colors.

An analysis of what this participant actually understood might provide insights into the textual processing behaviors of FL learners.

¶ <u>accurately understands</u>

1. NBC will do a show on the Virgin Mary.
3. Juan left and went to a town.
4. He saw an image of the Virgin Mary.
5. Something was built to protect Mexico.
8. Something had unique details.
4. Juan Diego saw a light radiating.
5. A temple was built.
5. Mary told him something.
6. Something about rose petals.
8. Juan Diego went and told someone.
7. Something happened to the petals of roses.
10. Image of Guadalupe exhibit in a city.
9. Something about investigations.
10. The number 10 and something about tourist attraction.
8. Something with bright and brilliant colors.

This participant actually recalled a number of elements, yet not enough to form a cohesive understanding of the storyline; thus, we can begin to see where deviations from the text occurred and how FL learners negotiated meaning between what is accurately understood and what is not understood. Note that this participant did attempt to follow the narrative sequence as it was presented in the text, which suggests that the participant had a good working memory. Interestingly, the recall begins with a reference to a magnificent glow of light and then ends with a reference to light again, suggesting an attempt at some type of cohesion.

DISCUSSION

The linguistically-based and cognitively-related sources of misunderstandings we observed in the recalls worked in concert to break down comprehension. From this analysis, we can say that when FL readers read a text about an unfamiliar topic, one they have little background knowledge to access for top-down processing, then they become more dependent on the language of the passage for interpretation, as suggested in Blau (1982). In other words, the reader will use a bottom-up approach to process the text. In so doing, the language of the text becomes more significant, and it is the language of the text that plays a greater role in creating conceptual hypotheses and also in confirming or rejecting them. When, however, the FL competence of the reader is also inadequate, the reader will resort to whatever language he or she can understand to construct meaning and fill in the gaps with propositions that work at that particular time, irrespective of whether they make sense or follow any cohesive thread. The result is a distortion of the original meaning, or what we have here referred to as misunderstandings.

In this study, the students' linguistic deficits were revealed in the misunderstandings that surface from complex sentence structures, false cognates, unfamiliar words, inattentiveness to grammatical markers, relative clauses, and prepositions. In paragraphs with complex sentence structures, the participants had problems parsing the sentences.

The following research may help explain why participants either omitted or misunderstood sentences with embedded structures. Research related to linguistic variables in reading comprehension suggests that FL learners parse sentences based on their native language parsing strategies, but those native language strategies may not be appropriate for the FL (Barry & Lazarte, 1995). Native writers of Spanish do not have necessarily the same writing style as English writers. English readers expect expository passages to develop in a linear fashion with little superfluous embedding in sentences, suggesting that every language may have particular writing preferences (Ka-

plan 1987). Barry and Lazarte note that "native writers of Spanish's exposi-
tions show a preference for long sentences with multiple embedded clauses
containing elaborations and digressions..." (p. 491).

In addition, Kintsch and van Dijk (1978) suggest that processing complex sentences puts a strain on the brain's short-term memory capacity that
in turn reduces recall of the information from the text at hand (p. 364),
which could be a partial explanation of why paragraphs 6 and 7 were often
omitted.

Berman (1984) argues that when FL texts contain complex sentence structures, learners will resort to controlled processing to find the propositional
content of the text. His findings indicate that "syntactic complexity might
be more of an impediment to grasping specific details than overall ideas"
(p. 146). His results, in addition to the previous ones, may help explain the
reader's behaviors toward complex sentences in the present study.

A potential explanation of the processing behavior described in this
study can also be found in the research on input processing (Byrnes, 1998;
Lee & VanPatten, 2003; VanPatten, 1996, 2003). VanPatten developed a
series of hypotheses and principles regarding input processing that appear
to be substantiated in the present study. According to VanPatten (1996),
FL learners process language, written or spoken, for meaning before form.
Within this hypothesis are three subsets of this hypothesis:

- Learners process content words in the input before anything else.
- Learners prefer processing lexical items to grammatical items for
  semantic information.
- Learners prefer processing more meaningful morphology before
  less meaningful morphology (VanPatten, 2003, p. 114).

In the second hypothesis, VanPatten (2003) contends that "[f]or learners to process form that is not meaningful, they must be able to process
informational or communicative content at no (or little) cost to attention"
(p. 114). Participants in this study processed content words and lexical
items, when they knew them, before forms.

In terms of syntactic structures, Pienemann's (1987) proposed psycholinguistic speech processing model may explain what might be happening
in processing complex syntactic structures in FL written texts. Pienemann
posits that FL speech processing is constrained by the word order developed by the learner for L1, and as acquisition in the FL increases, those
constraints relax to allow the possibility of different word orders. While
this model is proposed to explain speech processing, it also may explain
the difficulty native English speakers, such as the participants in this study,
had with processing written text with word orders that violated the Subject-
Verb-Object order typical of English—the participants' L1, but not the only

specified word order in Spanish. The FL learners in the present study may have been at the stage of acquisition where L1 word order constraints still dominated the hard wiring of the learners. The list of what participants did understand suggests they came from sentences with a Subject-Verb-Object word order or sentences on which they imposed an S-V-O word order.

We would expect that were we to analyze the misunderstandings of the other three texts in the original study, we would find similar linguistic-based patterns of misunderstandings, just not as many. We suspect that the other three texts enabled the readers to have a more balanced and interactive processing approach whereby top-down and bottom up processing worked simultaneously to achieve a more accurate understanding of the text, most likely due to such variables as familiarity with the text topic, facilitative rhetorical structures or textual voice, increased text length, or a combination of these variables. In the text we analyzed here, we can only conclude that either the lack of familiarity with the story of "La Virgen de Guadalupe" or the effects of text length (or both) played a major role in the comprehension, or lack thereof, of this text. For whatever reasons, this text was difficult to understand. When readers run into difficult texts of a similar profile, we now have some insights into the reading behaviors and processing approach.

In this study, when FL learners processed the text, they focused on key words and applied their expectations related to storyline development to produce a recall that was somewhat logical. Often, however, their reconstructions were not cohesive because of gaps in their processing of the information due to the heavy emphasis on controlled processing based on key words. In a study conducted by Maxim (2000), he documents somewhat similar processing behaviors of FL learners of German. He reports:

> Misreadings typically surfaced when students did not integrate the newly read material into the preceding events and behaviors. They viewed an event as being singular or independent of prior actions and did not attempt to make any connections between events within a particular text segment. (p. 79)

The recalls in this study also reflected a recollection of singular events independent of the previous recollection and/or the next ones (see the *Cognitively-related Misunderstandings* subsection). One misunderstanding could trigger numerous others, and the readers compensated by using whatever linguistic or cognitive knowledge they could, all depending on which one they accessed first. An analogy would have us recall the old-fashioned connect-the-dots children's workbooks, where dots are prearranged to form a picture. If, however, a number of dots are missing, the dots could be connected in different ways to create some type of image, but most likely a distorted one. Nevertheless, an image could be created by accessing the repertoire of previous images generated by life experiences and then, by using both the dots and the potential image, a picture could be forged that would be something, at least in the mind of the individual creating it. In this same way, students ended up with a recollection of textual elements, but a forced one. While the readers imposed some order or logic to what they recalled, often the recollections did not collectively form a cohesive and meaningful understanding of the text, but a distorted one.

Kramsch's (2003) research on cross-cultural misunderstandings indicated that institutions can impose a type of ideology on the discourse of speakers and that cultural differences can lead to misunderstandings. This led us to consider one other explanation for the lack of meaningful and coherent recalls generated by the students in this study. Academia has its own culture where there are teachers and students and there are certain expectations appropriate to each, individually and collectively. We asked ourselves if students' recalls could have been motivated by what they thought would be expected of them in an academic environment. In other words, if they honestly wrote down what they understood from the text, it might have been a series of words and phrases and maybe some pieces of the storyline, but certainly a limited amount of information. Turning in such a recall might not be what the students believe the teacher expects. A recall that reflects effort on the part of the student and shows some seemingly substantive level of understanding would certainly send a better message and would almost be expected within the rules of the academic culture. We call on future researchers to explore those possibilities as we endeavor to account for all potential explanations of how readers navigate discourse and negotiate meaning from it.

IMPLICATIONS

This study may have some practical implications for FL reading instruction. Doughty (1998) calls for "focus on form" researchers to investigate which forms are amenable to this approach to grammar instruction. The present research suggests that prepositions, conjunctions, and morphological and grammatical markers might benefit from "focus on form" instruction. Instruction that focuses on form-meaning connections may be useful with these particular items given that they may not be noticed by FL learners, since they may not be perceived as having much communicative value. Prepositions, conjunctions, and discourse markers, often referred to as "little words" (see Berman, 1984), are important in that they can mark intersentential and intrasentential relationships and often help build micro-level and macro-level propositions.

The misunderstandings stemming from false cognates suggest a need to draw attention to and create an awareness of (see Leow, 1997a) potential misreadings based on false cognates, perhaps through a sort of input flooding and use of positive evidence. Using false cognates correctly so that learners "notice" the correct meaning of the word may help learners detect them more quickly in written texts.

VanPatten (1996) offers concrete applications of input processing and grammar instruction. For some FL texts, the language features that interfere with comprehension and lead to misunderstandings could be integrated into reading instruction at the pre-processing and processing phase of comprehension and in non-traditionally configured ways. We will not know the effects of focus on form-meaning connections until we have accumulated enough empirical research to access its benefits. Until then, we should continue to explore which structures a focus on form-meaning connections would be amenable to such instruction.

We don't mean to say that reading should be converted into opportunities for grammatical instruction. Rather, that through reading, FL learners experience the relevance of grammar in the reading process, which could ultimately lead to a reduction in misunderstandings. Maxim's (2000) research and Beck et al. (1995) showcase engaging reconfigurations for FL reading instruction of this nature.

CONCLUSIONS

What started as a desire to understand what FL readers failed to understand has led to some important theoretical and practical considerations related to FL reading and input processing. Through an analysis of misunderstandings, we not only gain insight into the linguistic challenges of a text, we also gain insight into the cognitive processes FL learners adopt to negotiate meaning with the text. An analysis of FL reader misunderstandings could prove advantageous at all levels of SLA.

In the end, this study profiled the reading behaviors of FL learners of limited FL proficiency when faced with a culturally laced topic of which they have little knowledge. FL processing models and input processing may explain, in part, the reading behaviors of FL learners, but we are far from achieving a complete picture of either. We encourage additional qualitative and quantitative research that could lead to further insights into how FL readers negotiate meaning when they read and what kind of reading instruction would be most effective for them.

NOTES

1. Each idea unit received 1 to 3 points. Three points indicated that the pausal unit contained significant information; two points indicated that the pausal unit provided information that supported or expanded central information; and one point indicated that the pausal unit contained information not absolutely essential to the text. The scores were then converted into percentages from 0 to 100. The alpha reliability of the scores based on weighted pausal units was .91. Interestingly, only Text A had significantly higher recall scores than the other texts.

2. In scoring the recalls using the criteria of misunderstandings, the recalls were scored numerically from –1 to –3, based on the amount and type of information subjects misunderstood. A score of –1 indicated one or more misunderstandings, but not critical ones; –2 indicated a misunderstanding that was more critical to the storyline of the text but still allowed for some coherence in the storyline; and a –3 indicated the student had misunderstood the essential storyline of the text almost completely. The alpha reliability of the scores based on misunderstandings was .89. Intrarater reliability coefficients for all scoring procedures ranged from .90 to .94, $p > .05$.

3. Since we attribute the difficulty of this text, in part, to the lack of reference to existing cultural schemata in the FL readers, we think it important to explain the non-significant relationship between the recall scores and the topic familiarity questionnaire.

4. In the past, readability formulas typically assessed the comprehensibility of texts based on vocabulary difficulty and sentence length, but research indicates that they do not influence comprehension directly. Note in Table 5.1 that the readability level of the text with a significantly higher number of misunderstandings (Text B) than the others was rated Intermediate Level II, similar to Text C. The other two texts were rated Advanced Intermediate Level III, suggesting that Text B was lexically and linguistically as challenging as or less challenging than the other three texts. The readability rating used in this study was based on the Fry Readability Adapted for Spanish Evaluation (Vari-Cartier, 1981).

5. The shortened version of the text used in Leow's study was 384 words.

6. Wolf (1993) concludes, on the basis of her research, that more than one type of reading comprehension measure should be given to assess reading comprehension, and a relationship between the two established to strengthen the validity of the reading comprehension measures.

REFERENCES

Alexander, P. A., Schallert, D. L., & Hare, V. (1991). Coming to terms: How researching in learning and literacy talk about knowledge. *Review of Educational Research, 61,* 315–43.

Anderson, R. C., & Pearson, P. D. (1984). A schema-theoretic view of basic processes in reading comprehension. In P. D. Pearson (Ed.), *Handbook of reading research* (pp. 255–292). New York: Longman. (Eric Document Reproduction Service No. ED239236).

Barry, S., & Lazarte, A. A. (1995). Embedded clause effects on recall: Does high prior knowledge of content domain overcome syntactic complexity in students of Spanish? *Modern Language Journal, 79*, 491–504.

Beck, I. L., McKeown, M. G., & Worthy, J. (1995). Giving a text voice can improve students' understanding. *Reading Research Quarterly, 30*, 200–238.

Berman, R. A. (1984). Syntactic components of the foreign language reading process. In J. C. Alderson & A. H. Urquhart (Eds.). *Reading in a foreign language* (pp. 139–159). New York: Longman.

Bernhardt, E. B. (1984). Toward an information processing perspective in foreign language reading. *Modern Language Journal, 68*, 322–331.

Bernhardt, E. B., & Kamil, M. L. (1995). Interpreting relationships between L1 and L2 reading: Consolidating the linguistic threshold and the linguistic interdependence hypotheses. *Applied Linguistics, 16*, 15–34.

Blau, E. K. (1982). The effect of syntax on readability for ESL students in Puerto Rico. *TESOL Quarterly, 16*, 517–528.

Byrnes, H. (Ed.) (1998). *Teaching languages, literatures, and cultures, Vol. 1: Learning foreign and second languages: Perspectives in research and scholarship.* New York: Modern Language Association of America.

Carrell, P. L. (1983a). Three components of background knowledge in reading comprehension. *Language Learning, 33*, 183–207.

Carrell, P. L. (1983b). The effects of rhetorical organization on ESL readers. *TESOL Quarterly, 18*, 441–469.

Carrell, P. L. (1984). Schema theory and ESL reading: Classroom implications and applications. *Modern Language Journal, 68*, 332–343.

Carrell, P. L. (1987). Content and formal schemata in ESL reading. *TESOL Quarterly, 21*, 461–481.

Carrell, P. L. (1992). Awareness of text structure: Effects on recall. *Language Learning, 42*, 1–20.

Doughty, C. (1998). Acquiring competence in a second language: Form and function. In H. Byrnes (Ed.), *Teaching languages, literatures, and cultures, Vol. 1: Learning foreign and second languages: perspectives in research and scholarship* (pp. 128–156). New York: Modern Language Association of America.

Hague, S. A., & Scott, R. (1994). Awareness of text structure: Is there a match between readers and authors of second language texts? *Foreign Language Annals, 27*, 243–363.

Hoover, M. L. (1992). Sentence processing strategies in Spanish and English. *Journal of Psycholinguistic Research, 21*, 275–299.

House, J., Kasper, G., & Ross, S. (Eds.). (2003). *Misunderstandings in social life: Discourse approaches to problematic talk.* New York: Pearson Education.

Johnson, P. (1981). Effects on reading comprehension of language complexity and cultural background of a text. *TESOL Quarterly, 15*, 169–181.

Kaplan, R. B. (1987). Cultural thought patterns revisited. In U. Connor, & R. B. Kaplan (Eds.), *Writing across languages: Analysis of L2 text* (pp. 9–21). The Addison Second Language Professional Library Series. Reading, MA: Addison-Wesley.

Kintsch, W., & van Dijk, T. A. (1978). Toward a model of text comprehension and production. *Psychological Review, 85,* 363–394.

Kramsch, C. (2003). Identity, role and voice in cross-cultural (mis)- communication. In J. House, G. Kasper, & S. Ross (Eds.), *Misunderstandings in social life: Discourse approaches to problematic talk* (pp. 129–153). New York: Pearson Education.

Lee, J. F., & VanPatten, B. (2003). *Making communicative language teaching happen* (2nd ed.). *Directions in second language learning.* San Francisco: McGraw-Hill.

Lee, J.-W., & Schallert, D. L. (1997). The relative contribution of L2 language proficiency and L1 reading ability to L2 reading performance: A test of the threshold hypothesis in an EFL context. *TESOL Quarterly, 31,* 712–739.

Leow, R. P. (1997a). Attention, awareness, and foreign language behavior. *Language Learning, 47,* 467–506.

Leow, R. P. (1997b). The effects of input enhancement and text length on adult L2 readers' comprehension and intake in second language acquisition. *Applied Language Learning, 8,* 151–182.

Maxim, H. (2000, February 6). *Group work and misreadings: How students negotiate difference.* The Department of Foreign Languages and Literatures Symposium, University of Tennessee, Knoxville.

Pieneman, M. (1987). Psychological constraints on the teachability of language. In C. Wollman Pfaff (Ed.). *First and second language acquisition processes* (pp. 143–69). Rowley, MA: Newbury House.

VanPatten, B. (1996). *Input processing and grammar instruction: Theory and research.* Norwood, NJ: Ablex.

VanPatten, B. (2003). Cognitive characteristics of adult second language learners. In H. Byrnes (Ed.), *Teaching languages, literatures, and cultures, Vol. 1: Learning foreign and second languages: perspectives in research and scholarship* (pp. 104–127). New York: Modern Language Association of America.

Vari-Cartier, P. (1981). The readability and comprehensibility of Spanish prose as determined by the frase graph and the cloze procedure. State University of New Jersey–New Brunswick dissertation.

Wolf, D. (1993). A comparison of assessment tasks used to measure FL reading comprehension. *Modern Language Journal, 77,* 473–489.

Young, D. J. (1999). Linguistic simplification of SL reading material: Effective instructional practice? *Modern Language Journal, 83,* 350–366.

APPENDIX A
Para la NBC Estadounidense, La Virgen de Guadalupe es un 'Misterio No Resuelto'

1   Los productores y realizadores de la popular serie televisiva de la cadena estadounidense NBC-TV 'Misterios no resueltos' graban en la ciudad de México con artistas locales lo que se sabe de los orígenes del 'Milagro de Guadalupe,' informaron algunas fuentes de la industria.

2   La tradición dice que la imagen de la Virgen María quedó grabada en la capa de fibras de maguey de un indio azteca en el siglo XVI.

3   Según la leyenda, el 9 de diciembre de 1531, Juan Diego, uno de los primeros aztecas convertidos a la fe cristiana por los misioneros, iba camino de la ciudad de Tlatelolco, al norte de la ciudad de México, para asistir a misa.

4   Atraída su curiosidad por una luz brillante en la aurora, Juan se acercó, llamado por la Virgen María, rodeada de una luminosidad radiante.

Prueba de Veracidad

5   La aparición pidió a Juan Diego que en ese lugar sobre la falda del cerro del Tepeyac se construyera un templo en su honor, desde el cual ella extendería su protección al pueblo de México. Juan fue directamente a dar el mensaje al obispo, quien le pidió una prueba de la veracidad de 'La Señora del Cerro.'

6   Juan Diego regresó al mismo lugar y fue instruido por la aparición para que recogiera todas las rosas que pudiera encontrar en el lugar y que las pusiera dentro de su capa para llevarlas al obispo, los cual hizo.

7   Juan Diego regresó al mismo lugar y fue instruido por la aparición para que recogiera todas las rosas que pudiera encontrar en el lugar y que las pusiera dentro de su capa para llevarlas al Obispo, los cual hizo.

8   Aunque los detalles que los pintores han agregado en el transcurso de los siglos han palidecido y se han desprendido, los trazos y colores originales siguen tan nítidos y brillantes como al principio, hace más de 400 años.

Los Gobiernos Investigan

9   Las investigaciones ordenadas por sucesivos gobiernos mexicanos en 1556, 1666, 1756, y 1979 no han podido explicar el misterio de su factura y conservación.

10   La "imagen de Guadalupe" que se exhibe en la basílica del mismo nombre en la capital mexicana atrae cada año a 10 millones de visitantes. La Basílica de Guadalupe es la más popular del mundo católico después de la de San Pedro en el Vaticano.

11   ¿Qué es esta misteriosa imagen? ¿Una visión enviada por una deidad o pintada por un artista del siglo XVI cuya habilidad se adelantó a su tiempo? Este segmento, que será transmitido por la NBC esta temporada, tratará de explicar el misterio.

APPENDIX B
Translation

For NBC in the United States, the Virgin of Guadalupe is an 'Unsolved Mystery'

1   The producers and directors of the popular television series Unsolved Mysteries on channel NBC-TV will tape in Mexico City with local actors what is known about the origins of the 'Miracle of Guadalupe,' sources in the industry reported.

2   The legend says that the image of the Virgin Mary was engraved in the cloak of maguey fibers that belonged to an Aztec Indian of the 16th century.

3   According to the legend, on the 9th of December in 1531, Juan Diego, one of the first Aztecs to be converted to Christianity by the missionaries, was on his way to attend mass from the city of Tlatelolco, north of the city of Mexico.

4   His curiosity captured by a brilliant light in the aurora, Juan approached it, called by the Virgin Mary, who was surrounded by a luminous radiance.

Proof of Veracity

5   The apparition asked Juan Diego that in that very place at the lower slope of the hills of Tepeyac a temple be constructed in her honor from which she would extend her protection over the town of Mexico. Juan went directly to give the message to the Bishop, who asked for proof of veracity of 'The Lady of the Hill.'

6   Juan Diego returned to the same place and was instructed by the apparition to collect all the roses he could find around there and to put them in his cloak to take to the Bishop, which he did.

7   When Juan Diego unfolded his cloak in front of the bishop, the rose petals fell to the ground and an unfamiliar picture of the Virgin Mary appeared.

8   Even though the details that the painters have added in the course of the centuries have faded and detached, the original pieces and colors remain as vivid and brilliant as in the beginning, more than 400 years ago.

Governments Investigate

9   The investigations ordered by successive Mexican governments in 1556, 1666, 1756, and 1979 have not been able to explain the mystery of her workmanship and preservation.

10   The 'Image of Guadalupe' that is exhibited in the basilica with the same name in the Mexican capital attracts each year 10 million visitors. The Basilica of Guadalupe is the most popular in the Catholic world after San Pedro in the Vatican.

11   What is this mysterious image? A vision sent by a deity or painted by an artist from the 16th century whose skill was ahead of its time? This segment, which will be transmitted by NBC this season, will try to explain the mystery.

CHAPTER 6

"IT'S MADE TO MATCH"

Linking L2 Reading and Writing through Textual Borrowing

Hiram H. Maxim

ABSTRACT

Recent findings in L2 reading research cite the benefits to language development from supplementing reading with text-specific tasks that require learners to interact with the language in the text. One procedure for fostering
learner interaction with textual language is the appropriation of textual language into writing and speaking. To date, however, professional discussions
on textual appropriation tend to focus on the issues it raises regarding plagiarism rather than its potential facilitative effect on L2 language development.
In particular, little is known about how instructed adult learners themselves
view and work with texts as resources for their own learning. The paper addresses this issue, first, by arguing for a comprehensive reconsideration of textual appropriation's critical role in any language learning. It locates textual
borrowings within the gradual appropriation by all learners of a range of L2
textual features into their language use. For L2 learners and L2 instruction
this highlights a need to understand in explicit terms the type of language
that a specific text uses at the lexico-grammatical, sentential, and textual level.

Crossing Languages and Research Methods, pages 97–122
Copyright © 2009 by Information Age Publishing
97

Next, the paper outlines the pedagogical sequence implemented at the advanced level of a four-year integrated, content-based collegiate FL curriculum that explicitly attends to the textual language of the assigned thematically clustered readings. The paper then presents data from classroom observations, learner interviews, and analyses of learner writing to characterize how 6 advanced FL learners viewed and responded to this explicit instructional approach to narrow reading and writing development, focusing in particular on their approach toward and the type, degree, development of their textual appropriations across two semesters. The paper concludes with a discussion of the implications of this learner-based perspective on textual borrowing for L2 reading and writing instruction.

INTRODUCTION

In second language education, reading has long been seen as an important resource for language development. Already in the early days of formalized modern foreign language (FL) instruction in the late 19th century, reading in conjunction with the Grammar-Translation method was central to FL education. For better or for worse, the now infamous Coleman Report of 1929 solidified further the centrality of reading with its recommendation that reading be the primary focus and that reading proficiency be the most realistic goal in American FL education (see Bernhardt, 1998). To be sure, the second half of the 20th century, first with Audiolingualism and then later with Communicative Language Teaching, witnessed a noticeable move away from reading in favor of a strong focus on the development of oral competence, but even with this paradigmatic shift in FL pedagogy, reading remained an important modality, particularly in collegiate FL education with its strong emphasis on literary scholarship. Even as the lower levels of instruction in collegiate FL departments moved toward more communicative approaches to language instruction, upper-level classes continued to emphasize reading as the basis and point of departure for all subsequent language work. To the profession's detriment, this dichotomous approach to collegiate FL education has contributed to the institutionalization of the division between lower- and upper-level instruction that scholars have lamented for some time now (e.g., Byrnes, 1998; James, 1989; Kern, 2002; Maxim, 2006). However, in recent years, as learners, instructors, and researchers have experienced and documented the negative consequences of this structural division for language development, there has been growing interest in the profession, perhaps no more obvious than in the recent report by the Modern Language Association (2007), to address the current bifurcated system by integrating the two levels of instruction. Interestingly, rather than expanding the emphasis on oral competence into the upper levels, the focus has been almost exclusively on infusing the lower levels with richer content, thereby increasing the role for texts, textuality, and reading at those levels (see discussion in Byrnes, 2008).

Meanwhile, in another branch of instructed adult second language education, namely in ESL/EFL, the instructional context differs enough from collegiate FL education that reading has been and continues to be a central modality for language development. Collegiate ESL/EFL learners possess typically much more advanced language abilities than the average collegiate FL learner, and their coursework are designed usually as preparation for academic and discipline-specific study. As a result, students are exposed to academic texts from the outset and expected to use those texts as the basis for their writing and overall language development. Based on these instructional parameters, it is not surprising, for example, that the practice "reading-to-write" is associated most often with this educational context (e.g., Campbell, 1990; Carson & Leki, 1993). In the related sub-field of English for Academic Purposes (EAP) there has been additional work on the role of reading in language learning by focusing on genre as a potentially helpful construct for facilitating the academic preparation of second language learners (e.g., Johns, 1995, 2002). Defined here using Bhatia's (2002) characterization as "conventionalized communicative events embedded within disciplinary or professional practices" (p. 23), genre, because of its conventionalization, has proven to be an effective construct for understanding, analyzing, and teaching academic discourse as well as the discourse(s) of the dominant discourse communities.

A third development in second language education that has significant implications for the role of reading has been the emergence of sociocultural notions of language and language acquisition. Diverging from individualistic, psycholinguistic understandings of language, sociocultural approaches see language not as a preexistent meaning system but as arising from within a societal context. This emphasis on context reflects the influence of Hallidayan systemic functional linguistics on current thinking about language, for within functional linguistics central units of inquiry are context and the functional use of language within some context, i.e., the text (e.g., Halliday, 1994; Halliday & Hasan, 1989). Because of their functional, contextual nature, texts are thus seen not as individual entities but as genres that represent a socially situated and culturally embedded use of language in a specific context.

As reading gains prominence in the profession as a modality for fostering second language development, there are important questions to answer about the profession's approach to reading and its accompanying pedagogy. One immediate issue is the degree to which texts are to be seen as sources from which learners can borrow and appropriate language for their own use. This practice of textual borrowing or appropriation has been shaped largely by the attention it has received over the past 20 years from researchers and practitioners working with developing writers in academic ESL and EAP/ESP programs as well as in L1 university-level composition classes. Defined within this scholarship as the appropriate integration and documentation of other texts into one's own language use, textual borrowing understandably has been viewed from this perspective as a significant challenge for novice learners as they attempt to learn how to borrow from texts according to traditional western text citation practices and thereby avoid charges of plagiarism. As a result, much of the scholarship to date has had a twofold focus: first, to try to understand and explain textual borrowing practices of novice writers; and, second, to offer recommendations for revising instructional approaches to better accommodate the difficulties these writers face. To a large degree, dismissing the earlier notion that faulty textual borrowing results from either ignorance or intentional deception, researchers have identified a range of factors that help to clarify the behavior of developing writers. Kantz (1990), for example, attributes faulty textual borrowing to learners' inability to read rhetorically and thereby to identify the underlying argument of the source text. Without an awareness of the source text's rhetoric, writers then tend to represent the writing task merely as a reproduction of source material rather than a discussion of the source text's rhetorical context and problem. In her case study of one university-level ESL writer, Currie (1998) points out all the demands associated with a complex writing task and sees textual borrowing as a coping device in the face of the challenges in academic writing classes. Rather than focus on external variables affecting textual borrowing, Howard (1993) coins the term "patchwriting" to describe writers' "copying from a source text and then deleting some words, altering grammatical structures, or plugging in one-for-one-substitutes" (p. 233) and argues that this transitional stage of writing has important intellectual benefits for writers interested in acquiring academic-level discourse. Pecorari (2003) also sees patchwriting as a real and necessary stage for developing writers and argues that western text citation practices are not necessarily first and foremost on novice writers' minds during the writing process. In her later work, Pecorari (2008) argues that students' ability to incorporate source material appropriately into their own language use correlates closely with its pedagogical treatment in the classroom. Equipped with this more nuanced understanding of textual borrowing as a potentially beneficial practice for second language learners, the academic writing profession has been able to make much more concrete recommendations for revising pedagogical practice (Barks & Watts, 2001).

Based on this recent scholarship, an important next step in the research is to explore textual borrowing less as a product of the developmental process second language learners undergo toward becoming advanced users of the language and more as an important step in the reading process that can have a facilitative effect on second language acquisition, in general, and second language writing development, in particular. This chapter investigates textual borrowing as an essential link between reading and writing by, first, presenting an educational setting at the collegiate level in the United States in which texts and textual borrowing are considered central to language learning at all levels of instruction and, then, by examining the textual borrowing practices of six advanced learners of German over the course of one intensive semester of study (6 credit hours; 70 contact hours).

EDUCATIONAL CONTEXT

Defining Characteristics

Providing the context for exploring textual borrowing as an important link between second language reading and writing is the integrated undergraduate curriculum of Georgetown University German Department (GUGD). Because of its articulated integration of all levels of the curriculum into one unified approach to learning and teaching and thereby its eradication of the aforementioned division between lower and upper levels of instruction, the curriculum has achieved nationwide attention in the FL profession.[1] Serving as the unifying framework within the curriculum is a genre-based literacy orientation that has a threefold focus: (1) understanding the complex (con)textual nature of language use; (2) being aware of the conventionalized forms of language, i.e., genres, that are privileged in specific contexts; (3) and becoming facile at both reproducing and manipulating those genres for self-expression. Central to this type of literacy orientation therefore are texts, where texts are seen as genres that originate from and reflect a linguistic-cultural community that establishes a context as well as lexico-grammatical, discursive, social, and cultural boundaries within which meaning is made. In other words, learners' language use has to be appropriate based on the situated-ness of the text that they are producing as well as the situated-ness of the texts that they are drawing from to make meaning. In today's globalized and multilingual world in which texts appear in a range of media, literacy becomes an increasingly complex issue. As a result, scholars often use the plural form "literacies" in order to capture better the many different abilities that are necessary to function in public life (e.g., New London Group, 1996).

APPROACH TO TEXTUAL BORROWING

A genre-based literacy orientation has significant implications for the role of textual borrowing in the curriculum. A central underlying principle in this curricular approach is that there is a conventionalized nature to much language use. One of the early proponents of the notion of genre, Bakhtin (1986b), points out that conventionalization comes about because of the recurrent and intertextual nature of genre. Language users do not reinvent language for every communicative event; rather, they draw on stable and mandatory patterns of language use established in previous instantiations of that event. This notion of intertextuality, a term coined by Kristeva (1986) in her analysis of Bakhtin, has assumed a central position in the field of discourse analysis to assist in understanding the interpretation and creation of texts. Fairclough (1992), for example, stresses the dialogic nature of intertextuality discussed by Bakhtin to assert that a text both draws on prior texts and repositions them based on the current contextual factors. In a more recent discussion of intertextuality as it pertains to language learning, Johnstone (2002) describes the language learning process as progressing from "mimicking words, structures, purposes, and ways of talking that belong to other people" (p. 139) to appropriating these borrowed items according to one's individual way of meaning making. For Bakhtin (1986a) this dialogue between idiosyncratic forms of self-expression and generic, standardized patterns of language use was self-evident: "our speech, that is, all our utterances (including creative works), is filled with others' words, varying degrees of otherness or varying degrees of 'our-own-ness,' varying degrees of awareness and detachment" (p. 89).

Because of the curriculum's emphasis on the contextual and intertextual nature of language use, individual self-expression, long the hallmark of American education, is approached from a Bakhtinian perspective that considers our ability to express ourselves creatively dependent on our command of a specific context or genre; that is, the better our understanding of specific genres, the more freedom we have to use them. From this perspective, knowledge construction and ownership no longer resides in the individual but in a community of knowers who use, to use another Bakhtinian term, social languages. The task in a literacy-oriented curriculum, then, becomes facilitating the development of knowers by exposing them to a range of textual environments, by making them aware of how these environments use language to respond to particular contexts, and by encouraging their appropriation of others' language for their own purposes.

By drawing heavily on this literacy-oriented and genre-based approach to textual production and interpretation, the GUGD curriculum foresaw a different role for textual borrowing that identified it as an essential component of language learning. Much like Howard's (1995) recommendation of viewing patchwriting as a "pedagogical opportunity" (p. 788), curriculum planners implemented a text-based pedagogy that is centered around explicit attention to textual features at the discourse, sentence, and word level for the purposes of encouraging learner appropriation of these features for their own language production. The emphasis then, in contrast with much of the scholarship on textual borrowing, is not primarily on the appropriation of content but rather on particular language features that provide for opportunities to foster the construction of thought. Along the lines of Slobin's (1996) "thinking for writing," learners are encouraged in their interaction with texts to appropriate language that suits the meanings they seek to make. Choice and the agentive nature of textual production are therefore stressed while at the same time the limits placed on borrowing by generic conventions are clearly recognized.

Such explicit attention to textual borrowing elicits specific questions to research in this curricular setting:

1. How much do learners borrow from their reading?
2. What do learners borrow and why?
3. Do learners' borrowing practices change over time?

The following section presents a study of the textual borrowing practices of one segment of learners within the curriculum that will address each of these questions.

THE STUDY

Instructional Setting

Intensive Advanced German is a six-credit course (70 contact hours) open to students who have completed twelve credit hours of collegiate German (170 contact hours). The course met four times each week for a total of five hours and consisted of four thematic units that explored German cultural history from 1945 to the present as reflected in personal and public stories. For each unit, learners read 4–6 texts that served as carriers of content and models of language use. The instructional focus of each text was to facilitate the learners' understanding of the central content-related issues, the original purpose and context of the text, and the text's generic, sentential, and lexico-grammatical features. Particular emphasis was placed on directing students' attention to thematically marked lexico-grammatical features with a text, and the most prominent and consistent approach that was used throughout the curriculum for accomplishing that was the creation of semantic or word fields. Specific topics within each thematic unit were identified and then served as focal points for developing a field of semantically related lexico-grammatical features that were drawn directly from the thematically based texts (see a sample semantic field in Appendix A).

Each unit then ended with a writing task and a speaking task, both of which were formally assessed and were intended to provide a forum for students to apply the generic, content, and language knowledge they developed during the thematic unit to a specific situation. In the case of Advanced German with its focus on personal narratives framed against public events, each of the writing tasks asked students to tell a personal story against the backdrop of a major historical event and to draw on the content and language foci of the respective instructional unit. Table 6.1 provides an overview of the four instructional units and their accompanying writing tasks. One of the main criteria for successful completion of the language portion of the writing task was the use of theme-specific lexico-grammar. Students were thus encouraged once more to recognize that in order to successfully and appropriately discuss a particular theme, they needed to access topically relevant lexico-grammar from the readings.

The Participants

Six undergraduate learners of German (4 female; 2 male) participated in this study, three of whom had completed the previous level in the curriculum and three of whom had placed into the level based on the curriculum-based placement text (see Norris, 2004). Because this level of the curriculum is above the level required to fulfill the college's language requirement, all participants had chosen to take this course as an elective.

Data Sources

The data for analyzing the learners' textual borrowing practices consisted of the following: (1) the rough drafts of all four writing assignments; (2) transcribed interviews with each participant after submitting each rough draft (24 interviews); (3) periodic observations of the class; (4) periodic meetings with the instructor; and (5) instructional materials for the course.

TABLE 6.1 Instructional Units and Writing Tasks

Instructional unit	Writing task
Post-war Germany	Thank-you letter for care package
Divided Germany	Personal narrative about fleeing East Germany
Unified Germany	Public appeal
Contemporary multicultural Germany	Journalistic portrait of Vietnamese in Germany

Coding

Based on these varied sources, the researcher and two research assistants were able to determine which content-carrying words (i.e., nouns, verbs, adjectives, adverbs) had been borrowed from the course readings. Because the focus was on identifying the extent to which students drew on the readings for their own language production, any formulation that could be traced back to a source text or semantic field was considered a borrowed item rather than distinguishing between exact and close textual borrowings as Campbell (1990) did. Of course, a dogmatic approach to the role of textual borrowing in language learning would assert that all words in a learner-produced text are borrowed, but this study focused on just those items borrowed from materials in this course.

ANALYSIS

Quantitative Analysis

To provide a quantitative overview of the textual borrowings over the course of the semester, the mean and standard deviation of students' borrowings were calculated for each of the four writing assignments. Although the number of participants precludes a more sophisticated statistical analysis, the trend across the four tasks is worth noting. As Table 6.2 and Figure 6.1 indicate, when viewed collectively, the participants started off borrowing at a relatively high rate on the first writing task, decreased their borrowings slightly on the second task, then curtailed their borrowings noticeably on the third task before borrowing more on average on the final task (almost one-quarter of all content-carrying words) than on any of the previous

TABLE 6.2 Descriptive Statistics for Textual Borrowing (*n* = 6)

Student	Task 1	Task 2	Task 3	Task 4
1	15.8%	15.4%	3.4%	20.5%
2	16.3	7.6	6.1	18.1
3	18.5	12.6	2	23.9
4	16.7	18	7.6	20.8
5	17.1	13.5	10.7	25.8
6	12.5	13.2	3.9	24.3
Mean	16.15	13.38	5.62	22.23
SD	2.01	3.45	3.19	2.90

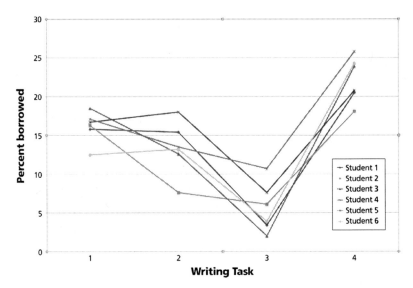

Figure 6.1   Percentage of content words borrowed across four writing tasks.

tasks. Because of the variation between and within tasks, a closer analysis of the pedagogy, the student performance, and the student response to the performance for each of the four tasks, will be conducted.

Writing Task 1: Thank-You Letter

The first thematic unit on immediate postwar Germany ended with the writing task that asked students to write a fictional thank-you letter to the donor of a care package sent at the end of war. Providing the content basis for this task, students read one descriptive text about care packages and four personal narratives about experiences that German speakers had at the end of the war (e.g., migrating from east to west; bartering on the black market; searching for loved ones). The approach to all five texts followed the same pattern of (1) reading the text outside of class to identify important themes and events; (2) reviewing the themes and events in class; (3) retelling the chronology of the story; (4) mining the text for salient lexical items that corresponded to semantic fields being developed in class; and (5) discussing the cultural significance of the text. By the end of the unit, the class along with the instructor had developed an extensive semantic field centered around the topic of "war's end" that included lexical items used to characterize the people (e.g., traumatized, homeless, hopeless), the cities (e.g., destroyed, bombed out, being cleaned up), and the political situation (e.g., to die, to be taken prisoner, to put down arms) at the end of the war (Appendix 1). In addition to the texts' serving to deepen students' understanding of the immediate postwar era, they also provided a context to practice the two targeted language features for the unit, expressing temporality and causality. Specifically, students worked with temporal phrases and subordinating conjunctions (e.g., before, after, when, because, whereas) to link events either temporally or causally. Following this work with texts and the targeted language features, students received a detailed description of the writing assignment (Appendix 2). Reflecting the genre-based nature of the curriculum, the assignment indicated the genre that students were asked to produce (a thank-you letter) and presented the features of the genre that students were expected to include according to three categories: (a) the nature of the task itself, in terms of the genre learners had to produce; (b) the content focus, in terms of the sources of information that were to be treated; and (c) the language focus, in terms of the features of German that were targeted at the discourse, sentence, and lexical-grammatical levels. All writing tasks throughout the curriculum are presented in this same tripartite format (see Byrnes et al., 2006 for detailed discussion of genre-based tasks).

In case students were unsure what kind of language to use in their thank-you letter, the detailed nature of the task sheet reminded them what to include and even what to borrow. For example, temporal and causal constructions as well as the semantic fields were listed as language foci that students should attend to. It is then perhaps not surprising that just over 16% of the content-carrying words in the six student-written performances were borrowed items. Specifically, the borrowings could be categorized as follows: (1) recently introduced constructions for expressing temporality or causality (e.g., the adverbs *therefore, because of that, one day, since the end of the war;* and conjunctions *after, before*); and (2) lexical items from the semantic fields (e.g., *to be taken prisoner, rubble, to reduce suffering*). In general, the students exhibited both a good understanding of the need to include the recently taught material in their writing and the ability to find lexico-grammatical items that suited their communicative purpose. The student perspective on this kind of writing task is reflected in the transcriptions of their interviews with the researcher.

Shortly after submitting the rough draft of the thank-you letter, each participant met with the researcher and discussed their approach to the draft, explaining their reasons for particular phasing and their overall reaction to the assignment. One student commented specifically about the type of textual borrowing encouraged in the GUGD and plagiarism:

> I had to rely heavily on the material, and we were specifically told that, if it fits best, we could directly quote from the text, because, you know, when you're learning, it's not plagiarism, you just learn the expressions. So, a lot of it came from the text and relying heavily on what was in the text, because otherwise I would have no idea what to say.

This student had thus come to terms with textual borrowing in this learning context and even recognized how essential it was to help him say what he wanted to say. Another student made the interesting comparison between writing in this course and writing in the first-year course when texts did not play such a central role:

> I remember, actually, first semester, we didn't have many texts, it was just kind of like, come up with it, and it was a lot more of a difficult experience, but with the texts, you already have an idea of what you're going to write and how you're going to say it, so it's a lot easier, so at that point, then, when you have the vocabulary and you have the phrases, then it's just a matter of coming up with your own idea and incorporating them into it.

Texts then were seen as a helpful resource for the learner, but it was clear that she saw the borrowed items as just vocabulary and phrases; the ideas came from her. Finally, a student commented on the benefits of the semantic fields (*Wortfeld*) that were emphasized so much in instruction:

> Especially with vocabulary, because you're already talking about the theme, you know, because it's made to match, and so having especially specific vocabulary there forces you, you know, it's a lot easier to just, you know, if I didn't have the *Wortfeld*, I could think of ways to say it, but probably a lot more primitive, but with the *Wortfeld*, it helps my vocabulary a lot, and actually gets me to be more creative in thinking about different ideas, instead of just what my ready vocabulary can give me.

Here was a student who has enough awareness about her own language abilities to see that the semantic field helped her express herself in ways that otherwise would not have been possible. She even used the expression "made to match" to characterize how certain wordings were tailor-made for certain situations and how there was no need to seek out alternative phrasing when the borrowed item met her communicative needs. The pedagogical challenge then becomes helping students recognize those wordings and providing a forum for them to use them.

Writing Task 2: Personal Narrative

The writing task in the second instructional unit on divided Germany asked students to retell a personal narrative about an escape across the East-West German border crossing from another perspective. Students started the unit by reading a descriptive text about the Berlin Wall that included specific terminology about the Wall (e.g., observation tower, border guard, no man's land, mine field). This reading served as the initial basis for a semantic field centered around the topic of the Wall and division. Students then devoted several class days to the personal narrative

"*Drei Freunde*" (Three Friends) that tells the story of three friends growing up in East Germany who go their separate ways to the point where one becomes the border guard who shoots at another as he is trying to escape across the border. The third friend who stays in the East narrates the story in hindsight. The pedagogical approach to this narrative followed the pattern used with the texts in the first unit, i.e., outside reading for major themes and events, in-class review of these themes and events, retelling of the chronology of events, developing the semantic field, and discussing the text's cultural significance. In terms of language foci, the class continued to study expressions of temporality and causality, but they also began learning expressions of opinion and argumentation (e.g., in my opinion, I believe that, from my perspective).

In addition, because this text was to serve as the model for the students' writing assignment, considerable class time was spent presenting and analyzing the text's narrative structure. Guided by Labov and Waletsky's (1997) seminal analysis of narrative structure (i.e., orientation—complicating action—evaluation—resolution), the instructor asked the students to identify the breaks in the text that marked the end of a section. The instructor then focused on the sentence that introduces the narrative's climax, the complicating action, "*Dann, eines Tages, geschah das Unfassbare*" (Then, one day, the unthinkable happened). Up until that point in the story the three friends had political differences, but that sentence indicated to the reader that something dramatic was about to happen. Reading a few lines more revealed the shooting on the border and the end of this once happy relationship (see Crane, 2006 for a detailed discussion of the text and the pedagogy).

The writing task was then to rewrite the narrative from the perspective of one of the other two friends. Specifically, the task sheet reminded students of the prototypical structure of narratives and the need for temporal phrases to organize the text. Students were also reminded to use vocabulary from the semantic field and the text to recreate the story.

This overt guidance on the task sheet combined with the explicit pedagogical focus on the text's structure resulted in a relatively high percentage of borrowed content words (13.3%) although not as high as on the first writing task. As expected there was significant borrowing from the semantic field and the text itself (e.g., to attempt an escape, difference of opinion) and the reuse of temporal phrases that had been reviewed in the unit. Less expected was the reappearance of lexical items from the first unit in some of the students' writing (e.g., to be taken prisoner, to order an execution). Perhaps most interesting was the students' response to the task requirement that they adhere to the structure of a personal narrative. Specifically, their decisions on how to introduce the narrative's complicating action reflected differing approaches to textual borrowing. With "Then, one day, the unthinkable happened" serving as the model, the six students opted for the following formulations:

S1: "Then, something so awful happened that it still bothers me to this day" (paragraph initial)

S2: "And now I will talk about that awful night" (paragraph initial)

S3: "One day Eberhardt and I fell in love with the same woman" (paragraph initial) . . . "The fatal night came, we tried to escape" (paragraph initial)

S4: "Tuesday came to an end and I was at home. Then, the unthinkable happened" (paragraph initial)

S5: "One day Max and I escaped over the border" (paragraph medial)

S6: "Then, one day, everything changed" (paragraph final)

S6's formulation represents the closest textual borrowing, but her decision to incorporate that sentence at the end of the paragraph arguably undercut its original intent of building suspense. In fact, except for S1 it could be argued that none of the students built up the same degree of anticipation in the reader as the original text. The students' comments about their borrowings shed some light on the choices they made. S1 recognized the need for drama with this sentence but also indicated her desire to deviate from the script:

> I like to deviate from the text, so you kind of learn to say the similar things different ways, and you know, make it your own. But I also wanted to make it the similar dramatic feeling, because it was so dramatic, like, that one incident was the key event.

How S1 preferred to appropriate language is what Bakhtin (1981) himself called "ventriloquation," the process of one voice's speaking through another voice, of taking a word and making it one's own. Representing a different approach to textual appropriation, S2 replied, "I had already borrowed some expressions, so I didn't want to borrow too much," to the question about why he had not borrowed more closely from the original. Therefore, going back to the source texts and the instructional materials to appropriate lexical items appeared to be largely a conscious and explicit act among the students.

Writing Task 3: Public Appeal

The writing task for the third unit on unified Germany required students to make a public appeal about a topic of their choosing. Serving as the textual model for this task were two public appeals delivered in East Germany in the fall of 1989, one right before the fall of the Berlin Wall and one right afterward.[2] Students followed the same reading process used with previous texts but spent additional time analyzing the structure and specific linguistic features of the two appeals. In particular, guided by worksheets that focused their attention on the text's organizational pattern, they identified two stages in these two texts that appeared to be necessary for achieving the genre's communicative purpose: a statement of the central problem and a solution to this problem. Furthermore, in conjunction with their instructor they identified six specific rhetorical devices in the two appeals that were effective in making a persuasive appeal: (a) imperative mood (e.g., Let's take the first path); (b) first-person plural pronominal usage to establish a feeling of togetherness (e.g., we, our); (c) direct address (e.g., my fellow citizens); (d) strongly connoted lexicon (e.g., political structures dominated by Stalinism, unreasonable conditions, a deep crisis); (e) modal verbs emphasizing the gravity of the situation (e.g., we cannot live like this anymore, we will have to endure this intolerable situation); and (f) parallel sentence structures to stress the urgency of the situation (e.g., we still have the chance . . . we still can fulfill the ideals . . .).

The assignment then asked students to write their own public appeal about a topic unrelated to unified Germany. They were encouraged to adhere to the structural and linguistic properties of the genre, but they understood that the semantic field would be completely different from that of post-Wall Germany. Not surprisingly, the degree of textual borrowing on this task was the lowest of the four tasks (5.6%). Therefore, rather than exploring the lexical borrowing that took place, an investigation of the structural and rhetorical borrowings that did or did not take place proved more interesting. In terms of the two stages identified as necessary for successful completion of the genre (Problem Statement and Solution), all students included both stages, but they differed in the degree to which they adhered to the rhetorical choices in the model texts. For example, the second appeal's first sentence (*Unser Land steckt in einer tiefen Krise*, Our country is stuck in a deep crisis) received significant instructional attention because it introduced the problem in such a forceful and effective way, and it obviously resonated with the students because it served as the basis for four of the six opening sentences:

S1: "Our education is stuck in a deep crisis"
S2: "Our wonderful cafeteria is stuck in a deep crisis"
S3: "Our city has a big problem"
S4: "Our country faces an epidemic that is quickly getting bigger"
S5: "Time at college is a critical time for the development of young people"
S6: "Today we live in a period of globalization with connections between countries and peoples unheard of in earlier times."

S5 and S6's decision to deviate from the textual model could be justified, but their opening arguably lacked the urgency and outrage of the model and the other four student versions.

A similar trend was evident in the way students presented the second obligatory stage of the appeal, the Solution. Once again, the second model text provided a compelling rhetorical device for motivating the audience to action. The solution was presented as an "either-or" proposition; those interested in addressing the problem could take one of two actions: the first one represented the choice of the authors and involved concrete action to combat the problem whereas the second one was a course of inaction and involved accepting the intolerable status quo. If there was any doubt about the authors' stance, then there was the clear recommendation to "take the first path" after the presentation of the two options. Specifically, the wording in the text followed the pattern: "Either we can...Or we will have to..." This particular formulation was emphasized in class as especially effective for a couple of reasons. First, by juxtaposing the preferred course of action with the consequences of taking no action and offering no other alternatives, the merits of taking action appear even more compelling. Second, the use of the first-person plural pronoun, which is repeated throughout both textual models, once again establishes a sense of commonality and togetherness that increases the likelihood that the reader will identify with the preferred course of action. Third, the choice of modal verbs strengthens the consequences of both options. The first option, "we can," the one preferred by the authors, is one that can be realized if action is taken. The authors and readers retain some agency in the face of this deplorable situation and are able to effect change if they act. The second option, meanwhile, "we will have to," indicates the loss of agency and alternatives; the existing power relations will remain in place and will continue to dominate the state of affairs with little chance of change. Fourth, in the second textual model the "either-or" statements are followed by the collective command "Let us take the first path" that, through its use of the first-person plural pronoun as well as the imperative mood, reaches out again to readers to include them in the movement and to urge them respectfully yet also unambiguously to take action. Last, the presentation of the two options is emphasized by printing the words "either" and "or" in bold-faced type and by inserting line breaks before and after each of the options. A result of this typographical emphasis is that the two options stand out to the reader both visually and rhetorically; they represent both the focal point and the climax of the genre by capturing what is at stake in unequivocal terms.

As a result of this pedagogical emphasis, all six students chose some version of this rhetorical device to present their solution to the problem:

S1: "Either we can . . . Or we will have to . . . Our demands

S2: "Either we can . . . Or students will have to . . . Let's take the first path"

S3: "Either Georgetown . . . Or students will have to . . . Let's take the first path"
S4: "Either we raise our own beef . . . Or we eat completely. Let's take the first path"
S5: "Either we can . . . Or we can . . . Let's take the second path"
S6: "Either we can . . . Or we can . . . Naturally we have to take the first path."

Nevertheless, only one of the six students (S1) followed the pattern exactly by using the same modal verbs and the same pronouns as the source text. Although it is beyond the scope of this chapter to evaluate the effectiveness of these samples, an initial assessment indicates that those who borrowed most closely from the source text ended up with more persuasive presentations of solutions to the stated problem.

In addition to the presentation of the two obligatory stages of the genre, students were also encouraged to include the specific sentence- and word-level rhetorical devices identified in the source texts and emphasized in instruction. Table 6.3 presents an overview of the extent to which the six students incorporated these six rhetorical devices. Whereas students' use of the imperative and modal verbs was consistent with that of the source text, their use of first-person plural pronouns and charged lexicon was noticeably less than that of the source text, thus reflecting the students' still developing abilities as readers and writers to recognize the importance of certain linguistic features in a text for contributing effectively toward the accomplishment of the text's communicative purpose.

The student comments on their rough drafts revealed an awareness of the importance of the text's rhetoric but also the challenges of addressing a topic that had not yet been treated in class. For example, one student stated outright, "The rhetoric of the text was very important," and "we were given a clear structure and then just plugged in information." Another com-

TABLE 6.3 Student Use of Rhetorical Devices in Public Appeal

Rhetorical device	Percentage of students to use device	# of examples of device in source text 2	Mean # of examples in student texts	Standard deviation among students
Imperative	100	1	3.00	2.19
1st person plural pronoun	100	16	12.50	8.02
Direct address	50	1	0.83	1.17
'Charged' lexicon	100	13	4.50	2.81
Modal verbs	100	5	4.67	2.07
Parallel structure	33	1	0.83	1.33

mented, "The structure helped a lot, but I had to use the dictionary a fair amount." A third student seconded that opinion by admitting his fondness for the semantic fields of earlier units, "I missed the *Wortfeld* this time...I wrote it first in English and then translated into German." While having a student in his fifth semester of German who still finds it necessary to write first in English is indeed troubling, it also sends the message to instructors and curriculum planners that there needs to be greater lexico-grammatical support for tasks that call on students to write on topics not covered in instruction.

Writing Task 4: Journalistic Portrait

The final unit of the course on contemporary multicultural Germany required students to write a journalistic portrait of Vietnamese in Germany. Students prepared for this task by reading a longer portrait of three other minority groups in Germany, statistics on immigration to Germany, and a feature article on the bureaucracy immigrants face when seeking citizenship. From these different texts the class developed semantic fields on the topics of immigration and citizenship. Class time was also spent analyzing the portrait genre for its attention to both the private and public sphere of the featured minority groups. In fact, the portrait begins with a personal account of a family representing the featured minority group, and then the discussion shifts to public officials who comment on the group's current situation both regionally and nationally.

The task itself was designed differently from the preceding three in that the information students gathered about Vietnamese in Germany came from three background texts that they had to read outside of class. There was only minimal discussion of the texts in class, and students were expected to glean relevant information on their own from the texts to use in their portrait. The assignment also asked students to present both a private and public image of Vietnamese in line with the model portrait analyzed in class. Last, as on all previous tasks, students were encouraged to draw on the semantic fields for relevant vocabulary.

As Figure 6.1 indicated, students borrowed on average more content-carrying words for this task than for any other (22.2%). On the one hand, this was not surprising considering that so much of the information for the portrait came from the three background texts; the students had no choice but to borrow. Students also borrowed from the semantic fields and they continued their earlier practice of borrowing lexical items from earlier units (e.g., stuck in a deep crisis, the unthinkable happened). On the other hand, the trend over the previous three tasks had been a reduction in the number of borrowings, causing one to speculate that perhaps students were becoming less dependent on source texts for lexico-grammatical support. However, as the performances on the previous task indicated, students were not comfortable with "saying it in their own words." They either missed the *Wortfeld* or resorted to the dictionary and translation.

This reliance on textual borrowing did not necessarily result in accurate borrowings, however. A closer analysis of the borrowings from the background texts indicates that, when left to borrow from texts that received limited treatment in class, students tended to truncate textual meaning based on their preconceptions about content, a characteristic of reading that first received significant scholarly attention thirty years ago (e.g., Anderson et al., 1977; Steffensen et al., 1979). As Table 6.4 illustrates, rather than rely solely on the information in the text, the students allowed their own notions about minorities in Germany to distort the meaning of the source texts. In the first example, the student concluded that the individual Tung did not know any German, but the source text only mentions what his first words in German were. In the third example, the student asserted that life in Vietnam was better than in Germany, but the source text only states that the return trip was "very good." A student suggested the opposite in the next example by saying that life in Germany was better than in Vietnam even though the source text only uses adjectives such as "good" and "nice" to describe Germany. As scholars, such as Bernhardt (1991) and Swaffar et al. (1991) pointed out years ago, these texts were not written for FL learners, and it is to be expected that misreading and truncation of meaning result. Thus, whereas the students had displayed an ability to

TABLE 6.4   Truncated Borrowings from Background Texts on Vietnamese

Source text	Student borrowings
"'Hello" and 'good night' were the first words that Tung could say in the foreign language	"Tung knew almost no German when he came to Germany"
"Huyen's father was a contract worker in the GDR. Back then he had to leave his wife and daughters in Vietnam"	"When her father came to the GDR as a contract worker, his family could come along"
"Tung described the return to Vietnam as 'very good'. What did he particularly like about it? 'Talking with my grandparents and friends'"	"Tung was much happier during this time than the time in Germany"
"The mother told Tung that Germany was 'good', that one can live there 'normally', that the people are 'nice'"	"His parents said that he will have a better future in Germany"
"Because contract workers had to wait a long time after unification for permission to bring their families, Huyen came just 4 years ago to Germany"	"After unification they waited for permission to join their father and because of the bureaucracy Huyen came just 4 years ago to Germany"

borrow lexical items effectively to express their own ideas, they still had difficulty comprehending without instructional assistance the ideas of others as expressed in texts.

The students' own comments after submitting this final writing assignment reinforced the notion that textual borrowing for them was a way to help them formulate their own ideas. One student stated, "When I could say it on my own and it would sound equally sophisticated, then I would say it on my own." Another echoed an earlier comment that reflected students' overt awareness of the extent to which they are borrowing from other sources: "If I find I am using too many words, I try to say it on my own." Finally, consistent with the findings on the role of depth of processing (e.g., Wesche & Paribakht, 2000) and degree of involvement (e.g., Hulstijn & Laufer, 2001) in vocabulary acquisition, a student acknowledged that the more instructional attention a lexical item received, the more comfortable she was using it: "The more it was reviewed, the more able I felt to use it."

Based on their comments and their borrowing practices, the students exhibited several interesting trends. To begin with, they had a general familiarity with and appreciation for borrowing in helping them "say it right," "to the point," and in a more "sophisticated way." At the same time, they had a desire to develop their own sophisticated voice in German and they did not feel bound to the source text for a specific formulation even in those instances when the text's formulation was arguably more effective. Nevertheless, they continued to see the importance of source texts for lexico-grammatical support, and they displayed a developing ability to borrow independently of instruction and to manipulate borrowed items from earlier units. As was just illustrated, the increased independent borrowing also highlighted even these advanced students' tendency to truncate textual meaning based on preconceptions.

CONCLUSION

In curricula that see reading as an important foundation for language development, textual borrowing takes on a central and unavoidable role. The situated and conventionalized nature of language use requires that learners attend to how language functions to make meaning in specific contexts. As the students' textual borrowing practices demonstrated, however, students need explicit guidance in identifying important items to borrow and in understanding how to use them. Furthermore, students need opportunities to use the borrowed items so that they can gradually make the items their own. However, students' reading comprehension at this level is by no means guaranteed, yet even when comprehension is satisfactory, students' reading remains primarily content-oriented in that their attention is not yet directed at language-related phenomena in the text. Therefore, whereas narrow reading allows learners to explore a topic in some depth, there needs to be supplemental instruction and assignments that will guide students in attending to language-specific features. Such was the goal of the genre-based writing tasks, but there could also be more fine-grained exercises that explore the linguistic realization of the textual message as a way to avoid misreadings. Such a text-based approach also places a premium on text selection so that students are exposed to not only the content but also the language and genre deemed appropriate for their level and communicative goals. In the end, texts are to be viewed as sources for meaningful language, and textual borrowing is the practice that allows readers and writers alike to access these texts and their rich textual language in order to advance their own language development.

NOTES

1. For further information on the GUGD curriculum visit http://german. georgetown.edu
2. The first appeal was delivered by Stefan Heym in early November 1989 on the Alexanderplatz in East Berlin. The second appeal, entitled *Für unser Land* (For our Country), appeared in late November 1989 and later in a volume edited by Borchert, Steinke, and Wuttke (1994).

REFERENCES

Anderson, R. C., Reynolds, R. E., Schallert, D. L., & Goetz, E. T. (1977). Frameworks for comprehending discourse. *American Educational Research Journal, 14*(4), 367–381.

Bakhtin, M. M. (1981). *The Dialogic imagination: Four essays by M. M. Bakhtin* (C. Emerson & M. Holquist, Trans.). Austin: University of Texas Press.

Bakhtin, M. M. (1986a). *Speech genres and other late essays* (V. W. McGee, Trans.). Austin: University of Texas Press.

Bakhtin, M. M. (1986b). The problem of speech genres (V. W. McGee, Trans.). In C. Emerson & M. Holquist (Eds.), *Speech genres and other late essays* (pp. 60-102). Austin, TX: University of Texas Press.

Barks, D., & Watts, P. (2001). Textual borrowing strategies for graduate-level ESL writers. In D. Belcher & A. Hirvela (Eds.), *Linking literacies: Perspectives on L2 reading-writing connections* (pp. 246–267). Ann ArborI: University of Michigan Press.

Bernhardt, E. (1991). *Reading development in a second language: Theoretical, empirical, and classroom perspectives.* Norwood, NJ: Ablex.

Bernhardt, E. (1998). Sociohistorical perspectives on language teaching in the modern United States. In H. Byrnes (Ed.), *Learning foreign and second languages. Perspectives in research and scholarship* (pp. 39–57). New York: MLA.

Bhatia, V. K. (2002). A generic view of academic discourse. In J. Flowerdew (Ed.), *Academic discourse* (pp. 21–39). Harlow, UK: Longman.

Byrnes, H. (1998). Constructing curricula in collegiate foreign language departments. In H. Byrnes (Ed.), *Learning foreign and second languages: Perspectives in research and scholarship* (pp. 262–295). New York: MLA.

Byrnes, H. (2008). Perspectives. *Modern Language Journal, 92*(2), 284–287.

Byrnes, H., Crane, C., Maxim, H. H., & Sprang, K. A. (2006). Taking text to task: Issues and choices in curriculum construction. *ITL—International Journal of Applied Linguistics, 152,* 85–110.

Campbell, C. (1990). Writing with others' words: Using background reading text in academic compositions. In B. Kroll (Ed.), *Second language writing: Research insights for the classroom* (pp. 211–230). New York: Cambridge University Press.

Carson, J. G., & Leki, I. (Eds.). (1993). *Reading in the composition classroom: Second language perspectives.* Boston: Heinle.

Crane, C. (2006). Modelling a genre-based foreign language curriculum: Staging advanced L2 learning. In H. Byrnes (Ed.), *Advanced language learning. The contributions of Halliday and Vygotsky* (pp. 227–245). London: Continuum.

Currie, P. (1998). Staying out of trouble: Apparent plagiarism and academic survival. *Journal of Second Language Writing, 7*(1), 1–18.

Fairclough, N. (1992). *Discourse and social change.* Cambridge, UK: Polity.

Halliday, M. A. K. (1994). *An introduction to functional grammar* (2nd ed.). London: Edward Arnold.

Halliday, M. A. K., & Hasan, R. (1989). *Language, context, and text: Aspects of language in a social-semiotic perspective.* Oxford: Oxford University Press.

Howard, R. M. (1993). A plagiarism *Pentimento. Journal of Teaching Writing, 11*(3), 233–246.

Hulstijn, J., & Laufer, B. (2001). Some empirical evidence for the involvement load hypothesis in vocabulary acquisition. *Language Learning, 51,* 539–558.

James, D. (1989). Re-shaping the 'college-level' curriculum: Problems and possibilities. In H. S. Lepke (Ed.), *Shaping the future: Challenges and opportunities* (pp. 79–110). Middlebury, VT: Northeast Conference.

Johns, A. M. (1995). Teaching classroom and authentic genres: Initiating students into academic cultures and discourses. In D. Belcher & G. Braine (Eds.), *Academic writing in a second language: Essays on research and pedagogy* (pp. 277–291). Norwood, NJ: Ablex.

Johns, A. M. (2002). *Genre in the classroom: Multiple perspectives.* Mahwah, NJ: Lawrence Erlbaum.

Johnstone, B. (2002). *Discourse analysis.* Malden, MA: Blackwell.

Kantz, M. (1990). Helping students use textual sources persuasively. *College English, 52,* 74–91.

Kern, R. (2002). Reconciling the language-literature split through literacy. *ADFL Bulletin, 33*(3), 20–24.

Kristeva, J. (1986). Word, dialogue and novel. In T. Moi (Ed.), *The Kristeva reader* (pp. 35–61). Oxford: Blackwell.

Labov, W., & Waletsky, J. (1997). Narrative analysis: Oral versions of personal experience. *Journal of Narrative and Life History, 7*(1–4), 3–38.

Maxim, H. H. (2006). Integrating textual thinking into the introductory college-level foreign language classroom. *Modern Language Journal, 90*(1), 19–32.

MLA Ad Hoc Committee on Foreign Languages. (2007). Foreign languages and higher education: New structures for a changed world. *Profession 2007,* 234–245.

The New London Group. (1996). A pedagogy of multiliteracies: Designing social futures. *Harvard Educational Review, 66*(1), 60–92.

Norris, J. M. (2004). *Validity evaluation in foreign language assessment.* Unpublished doctoral dissertation. University of Hawai'i at Manoa.

Pecorari, D. (2003). Good and original: Plagiarism and patchwriting in academic second-language writing. *Journal of Second Language Writing, 12,* 317–345.

Pecorari, D. (2008). *Academic writing and plagiarism: A linguistic analysis.* London: Continuum.

Slobin, D. I. (1996). From "thought and language" to "thinking for speaking." In J. J. Gumperz & S. C. Levinson (Eds.), *Rethinking linguistic relativity* (pp. 70–96). Cambridge: Cambridge University Press.

Steffensen, M. S., Joag-Dev, C., & Anderson, R. C. (1979). A cross-cultural perspective on reading comprehension. *Reading Research Quarterly, 15,* 10–29.

Swaffar, J. K., Arens, K. M., & Byrnes, H. (1991). *Reading for meaning: An integrated approach to language learning.* Englewood Cliffs, NJ: Prentice-Hall.

Wesche, M. B., & Paribakht, T. S. (2000). Reading-based exercises in second language vocabulary learning: An introspective study. *Modern Language Journal, 84*(2), 196–213.

APPENDIX A
Semantic Field for the Topic "War's End"

WAR—WAR'S END
The war is over
Day of victory and liberation

POLITICS/POWER

To win = to triumph	To lose = to be conquered
The victor / the conquerer	To collapse in death and rubble
	to surrender
	cease fire / to put down one's arms
	to sign the surrender agreement
	to be sentenced to death

To denazify the Germans

CITIES:
Destruction
To destroy
Rubble and ashes—to lie in rubble and ashes
Ruins—to lie in ruins
To divide the city into sectors

PEOPLE:
Sad, hopeless, to look lonely, homeless

women	Männer
to clear away the war rubble	To come home traumatized
to clean up the city	To be captured
to carry roof tiles	To be taken prisoner
to sweep streets	To end up in prison
to take care of the children	To be dead
to build up the homes again	To kill someone
reconstruction	To die
to be raped	To be a victim
a rubble woman	

APPENDIX B

Advanced German
Thema 1 (Post-War Germany)
Writing task 1

Task: Thank-you letter
Imagine that it is 1946 and that you live in decimated Germany. You just received a care package from the USA and want to write letter of thanks. The content and style depend on whether you know the addressee. Think about who this person is and how you should address her/him. A thank-you letter consists of the following parts:

- Salutation and date;
- Reason for writing;
- Presentation of your situation (past, present, future);
- Logical conclusion (including signing off and signature).

Content
Basis for your letter are the texts read in class. These texts offer a great deal of information and vocabulary about the people and the situation at the end of the war.
You should address the following aspects in your letter:

- What you are thankful for
- What you experienced in the war
- What your living conditions are like
- How the care package improved your situation
- What your plans and hopes for the future are

The accuracy and depth of the content is extremely important

Language Focus:
Discursive level:

- narrate: chronological portrayal of your situation during and after the war
- explain: why the care package reduced your suffering
- coherent division of the letter into paragraphs

Sentence level:

- Temporal phrases (*e.g.,. at first, then, one day, in the year, since war's end*) and subordinate clauses that begin with *after, before, when*
- Subordinate clauses for justifying (e.g., *because, therefore*)
- Position of the verb, particularly in subordinate clauses
- Gender; case; case after preposition; subject-verb agreement

Word level:

- Relevant vocabulary from the texts and semantic fields
- Spelling, punctuation, capitalization

Writing process:
Preparation sheet, first draft due on _____ .
Final draft due on _____ .
Length: 1.5 pages, double-spaced

Grading criteria:
  The three categories of task, content, and language focus are weighed equally. The overall grade is an average of the three grades for these categories. You can improve your grade for the second draft maximally up to 6 points (very good revision: improvement by 6 points, e.g., from B– to B+; good revision: improvement by 3 points, e.g., from B to B+; satisfactory or poor revision: no improvement of the grade).

CHAPTER 7

COMPREHENSION AND COMPENSATORY PROCESSING IN ADVANCED L2 READERS

Alan McMillion and Philip Shaw

ABSTRACT

This study focuses on first year biology students at Stockholm University who are assumed by the Swedish university system to be able to read textbooks in English. These students are compared with first year biology students at two British universities, all of whom were first language (L1) readers of English. Several components of reading comprehension are compared. The Swedish readers are subdivided on the basis of a reading comprehension test into two subgroups, referred to as the 'very' advanced and the 'less' advanced second language (L2) groups. Other measures of reading skill are then used to compare the two Swedish groups with each other and with the L1 group.

The results indicate that the very advanced Swedish readers of English are fully comparable to the L1 readers on reading comprehension and inferencing tasks. However, these very advanced L2 students were nonetheless somewhat weaker on vocabulary, recall, and word recognition (lexical decision) tasks when compared to the L1 students. It is speculated that the L2 readers gener-

Crossing Languages and Research Methods, pages 123–146
Copyright © 2009 by Information Age Publishing
123

ally use inferencing, in the form of general world knowledge and bridging inferences, as a means of compensating for lack of automaticity in low level processing. The less advanced Swedish readers, who comprise the majority of the L2 students, were considerably weaker than the very advanced students on all tests, suggesting that these students may in fact be considerably disadvantaged in having to read course material (in this case biology) in English.

A coefficient of variation was calculated for the word recognition speed test and the sentence coherence recognition speed test as an indicator of automaticity for the L1 group and the L2 group as a whole. For word recognition there was a clear difference, but for sentence coherence the difference was less apparent. A possible explanation is that some of the sentence coherence test items were contrary to expectation and forced the L1 subjects to slow down and consciously work out whether the sentence was coherent or not.

The general conclusions are (1) that the majority of Swedish students do not meet the English reading expectations of the university system, and (2) a minority of the Swedish students, although they had lower scores on vocabulary and recall tasks and less automaticity on the response-time tasks than the L1 readers, seemed to compensate for these weaknesses with inferencing skills, allowing them to achieve comparable reading comprehension product to the L1 readers.

INTRODUCTION

Within higher education the use of English has been increasing in many countries in Europe and Asia where it is neither the majority nor an official language. Even where the majority of students and faculty are not L1 English users, English is one of the languages of lectures, seminars, and discussions between students and faculty. It is also very often the language of textbooks. A recurring question that many educators in these countries are asking is the extent to which the students that do not have English as their L1 are disadvantaged in their university studies. Although production skills in English are important for these students, it would seem that receptive skills, both reading and listening skills, are the most crucial for success at the university. Clearly, the level of receptive proficiency among students must be quite high in order for them to be able to follow the course work adequately.

This chapter will look at the reading and comprehension skills of what we will designate as the advanced L2 reader. An advanced L2 reader may be characterized as such on the basis of various criteria, e.g., scores on reading comprehension tests or achieving satisfactory results in relevant courses in the L2 (e.g., in upper secondary school). For our purposes, an advanced L2 reader will be operationalized as one whose accuracy score is within two standard deviations of the L1 mean on a comprehension test, where the L1 counterparts are L1 readers with very similar educational and social backgrounds. Some L2 readers may in fact be characterized as having "near-native" or "native-like" receptive proficiency, which would presumably constitute a higher and distinct level (e.g., Hyltenstam, 1988). However, since the meaning of the term "near-native" is often left unoperationalized and linked to production, its use as a category of L2 receptive proficiency is not entirely clear.

The pre-theoretical notion of advanced readers of L2 English is especially interesting for several reasons. First, as mentioned above, there is a large and growing number of L2 English students in countries around the world reading English textbooks as part of their university courses (Graddol, 2006). It would be very helpful for university educators to know just how well the reading comprehension product and processing of these students compare to that of L1 students reading the same texts. Second, research has shown (e.g., Shaw & McMillion, 2008) that only a minority of these students have comprehension product scores that are clearly in the L1 range of performance. In addition to product scores, processing differences are particularly relevant in comparing the L1 and L2 readers, and two broad questions spring to mind: (1) how do the reading processes of highly proficient L2 readers compare to those of L1 counterpart readers, and (2) how do the reading processes of these highly proficient L2 readers compare to those of L2 readers whose product scores are considerably below those of L1 counterpart readers?

Pre-theoretically we can speak of at least three "advanced" English L2 reading populations: (1) the broad population of non-L1 English students who are assumed to read English textbooks as part of their university coursework, (2) a subset of this group who achieve reading proficiency scores in the range of equivalent L1 readers (within 1 SD of the mean of the L1 scores), and (3) the subset of the broad group who achieve reading proficiency scores below 1 SD but within 2 SDs of the L1 readers' mean. For convenience, the first broad group will simply be referred to as "advanced," the high-scoring subgroup as "very advanced," and the lower scoring subgroup as "less-advanced."

The boundaries of the two L2 subgroups will be inherently vague and some arbitrary choices concerning where to draw the boundaries is unavoidable. Gernsbacher and St. John (2001), for example, use the upper third and the lower third of a group of L1 comprehenders based on the Multi-Media Comprehension Battery to create groups of more and less-skilled L1 comprehenders. Nonetheless, regardless of how one draws the category boundaries, our data indicate that it is likely that only a minority of L2 readers are clearly in the L1 range, with the majority considerably below the L1 means. One immediately evident implication is that the majority of L2 students, though certainly not all, could possibly benefit from various kinds of L2 reading comprehension boosting activities, e.g., comprehension strategies instruction, vocabulary instruction, etc. (Snellings, van Gelderen, & de Glopper, 2002).

Although the larger advanced L2 group is often the target group in discussions concerning L2 English readers, this paper will focus on the very-advanced and the less-advanced groups as individual populations. Possible reasons that explain why these groups are particularly interesting and include the following:

1. Relatively less research has been carried out on the advanced group compared to beginner and intermediate levels of L2 readers (the focus often being on L2 acquisition/learning rather than L2 use).
2. Insights into processing differences in the very-advanced group compared to the less-advanced group might inform us about potentially useful pedagogical intervention to bolster the less-advanced students.
3. It is not entirely clear what factors allow some L2 readers to become very-advanced and even "native-like" while others, with presumably the same L1 and L2 reading experience, are measurably below the very-advanced level of reading proficiency.

THEORETICAL BACKGROUND

An initial hypothesis might be that advanced L2 readers are differentiated from comparable L1 readers by the same component skills that differentiate good from poor L1 readers. Some of the reading components claimed to be weaker in poor L1 readers include the following (Long, Johns, & Morris, 2006; McNamara, de Vega & O'Reilly, 2007).

1. Word processing (they are often slower)
2. Inferencing, particularly regarding topic.
3. Integrating incoming information with preceding discourse.
4. Constructing bridging inferences.
5. Resolving anaphors (differently).

With the exception of word processing, the weakest components of poor L1 readers are higher level, coherence-related processes. Since it can be assumed that, overall, advanced L2 readers do not differ systematically in nonlinguistic aspects of L1 reading skills (such as inferencing skills or working memory span), or in motivation or personality, from L1 readers, they presumably vary in these skills in the same way as L1 readers. They are likely to have different background knowledge, particularly cultural knowledge, but this is a reflection of cultural, not linguistic, differences, and is only relevant in tasks dealing with particular types of topics. After all, two L1 users of the same language can easily vary in cultural or background knowledge. Where cultures are very different, we may anticipate differences in reading practices and strategies, but in the case to be discussed the cultures are very similar and there is no evidence of systematic differences on this level. On average, therefore, advanced L2 readers should be at least comparable with L1 readers in terms of extra-linguistic skills. This implies that the relevant differences between the mean performances of L1 and advanced L2 readers would be primarily due to linguistic factors, and therefore that only the first of the differences listed above would be relevant.

This analysis is consonant with the three groups of component skills conceptualized by workers in the ongoing NELSON project: (1) language knowledge, (2) speed of access to language knowledge, and (3) metacognitive knowledge (Fukkink, Hulstijn, & Simis, 2005). Metacognitive knowledge is often regarded as representing language-independent, higher-order processing skills that are transferable (normally with positive results) from L1 to L2 reading.

Bernhardt (2005) proposes a compensatory perspective on L2 proficiency, claiming that knowledge sources (particularly L1 literacy and L2 knowledge) is not strictly additive but interact synergistically: "the higher the L1 literacy level, the more it is available to buttress impoverished second language processes,... the more word knowledge is developed, the more it frees up resources to operate on more complex syntactic patterns, and so forth" (p. 140). L1 literacy can be conceptualized as a set of habits, behaviors and strategies utilized for processing texts and acquired while learning to reading in L1. In addition to processing behaviors L1 literacy should include strategies for dealing with the various kinds of obstacles and problems that occur in text processing. In other words, L1 literacy would include behaviors and strategies for dealing with problems conditioned by inefficient processing and lack of textual coherence. What is transferred from L1 reading to L2 reading, then, is not only those L1 processes that are applicable and efficient but also those behaviors and strategies used to handle processing difficulties (thereby improving the efficiency of less-efficient component processes).

Although Bernhardt (2005) discusses the transfer of literacy skills, such as alphabet recognition, vocabulary recognition and access, text structure, and expectations concerning text structure, she does not analyze them into component processes (p. 140). It would seem that these skills occur at different levels of the reading process. Letter and word recognition are certainly low-level skills where automated recognition processes are easily transferred from the reading of L1 to the reading of L2 texts. For cognate languages such as Swedish and English, this does not constitute an obstacle for the L2 reader (although Swedish does have three letters, å, ä and ö which English lacks). Vocabulary recognition and lexical-semantic access are processes that could present L2 readers with obstacles to smooth reading, either because their L2 vocabularies do not include many of the words in a text or that their meanings are not well entrenched or too vague with insufficient supporting context. This is also a problem for weaker L1 readers. Bernhardt's conception of compensatory processing involves the quite broad categories of L1 literacy and L2 knowledge and unexplained variance, e.g., that good domain knowledge can compensate for weaker L2 knowledge. While this is certainly true, the complexity of reading should remind us that conceptual simplifications must be handled with care. It may not be L1 literacy per se that compensates for weak L2 knowledge, but a set of processes, some highly automated, some less so or even explicit, de-clarative, and conscious, that are intricately interwoven (Walter, 2007). The contribution of L1 literacy, for example, may be viewed as a set of higher level, text-modeling processes that were learned when speakers learned to read their L1. L2 knowledge will certainly include L2 specific word and grammatical processes, but many of these may have been transferred early from L1 processing. (Hence, concerning initial learning of an L2 Bern-hardt [2005, p. 139] says "there is already some literacy knowledge on the part of all readers especially from cognate languages.")

Walczyk (2000) makes several predictions in his model of compensatory processing concerning weaker and stronger L1 readers. Walczyk claims that the interplay between automatic and control processes in reading is intri-cate and variable, but given the range of individual variability in many sub-skill reading processes, he argues that readers use a variety of strategies and behaviors to compensate for inefficient automatic processing. Walczyk's model (Compensatory-Encoding Model) predicts that the range of read-ing product scores among L1 readers of a similar educational background will be fairly narrow, but, because of less efficient processing, weak readers will need more time to reach this level of comprehension product. It is not clear what Walczyk means by 'comprehension', but one can assume that it is intended to refer to the uptake of the textbook writers' intentions about the meaning of the texts. (See van den Broek, Risden, & Husebye-Hartmann, 1998; van den Broek et al., 2002, concerning standards of coherence.) Of relevance here is the question of the extent to which poor L1 readers can be compared to advanced L2 readers on any parameter other than speed.

The field often designated "discourse processes" (Zwaan & Radvansky, 1998) has greatly advanced our general understanding of this level of processing, and since researchers in this area primarily focus on higher level reading processes (e.g., coherence building, inference creation), even understanding of reading processing has been enhanced by this line of research. It is unclear why relatively less L2 research has focused on these higher level processes, unless there is a general belief among L2 researchers that once decoding and parsing are complete, L2 discourse processing proceeds along the same processing paths as L1 discourse processing. Koda (2004) devotes a chapter to discourse processing, yet there are only a handful of references to studies focusing specifically on L2 discourse processing. Nevertheless, Koda takes the position that L1 and L2 text comprehension processes (and products) are fundamentally different (p. 123), and that models of L2 comprehension can be developed by probing these differences.

In the current paper, several threads will be drawn together to support the view that very-advanced L2 readers may be compensating for inefficient lower level processes via higher, conscious, levels of processing, but will nonetheless tend to slow down the whole-reading process. On the surface it might seem reasonable to assume that many aspects of advanced L2 reading will be similar or identical to corresponding L1 aspects of reading and that strategies and behaviors for overcoming deficient processing should be likewise similar. There are undeniably some similarities between poor L1 readers and advanced L2 readers, such as smaller vocabulary breadth and depth, slower word recognition, weaker collocational knowledge, and perhaps slower parsing. However, the strategies and behaviors for overcoming deficits may be quite different in L1 and L2. A good L1 reader will have many lower-level processes highly automated, while even an advanced L2 reader will not have automated these lower level processes to the same degree. The L2 reader will already be a more-or-less competent L1 reader when he or she begins learning the L2. It is therefore likely that such readers have learned to rely on background knowledge of various kinds as well as inferencing to fill in gaps which the L2 reading process has left open.

In short, we can postulate two main differences between the advanced L2 readers and poor L1 readers: (1) many L2 readers are good readers in their L1 and consequently can be assumed to have efficient L1 reading strategies and behaviors, which can be transferred to L2 reading, for dealing with problems such as lack of lexical knowledge or unclear textual cohesion; (2) L2 readers have, through learning to read the L2, likely developed strategies for relying on higher-level processes, such as accessing background knowledge and inferencing. The results described below seem to support at least the latter.

The issue of differences between the very-advanced and the less-advanced L2 groups can now be formulated along the following lines: do the less-advanced L2 readers show the same differences as the very-advanced L2 readers when compared to the L1 readers, only more so, or do they differ along other dimensions?

RESEARCH QUESTIONS

Our primary aim is to compare L1 readers' reading product and processing with those of the very-advanced and the less-advanced L2 readers. Just as the broad group of advanced L2 readers shows considerable internal variation, the L1 groups that were used as benchmarks also consist of high and low performance students. For current purposes, however, it is the mean of the L1 readers that will be used to classify the advanced L2 readers.

In comparing the L1 with the L2 groups on the one hand, and the very-advanced L2 group with the less-advanced L2 group on the other, some of the relevant research questions include the following:

1. How great is the variance for the product scores among the various groups?
2. What processing differences can be found between the L1 readers and the very-advanced L2 readers, e.g., speed and efficiency measures?
3. What processing differences can be found between the very-advanced L2 readers and the less-advanced L2 readers? Are the very-advanced simply faster?
4. How do the two L2 subgroups compare with the L1 group on different tasks, e.g., the standard comprehension tests and reading for recall, the latter which implies more robust modeling of the text?

METHOD

Participants

This chapter is based on studies done at Stockholm University during 2007–2008. The groups of informants include 100 first year Swedish biology students at Stockholm University and 49 British first year biology students at Reading and Edinburgh Universities. All the subjects for this study had roughly the same educational background, in that all had completed secondary education to similar levels, none had much tertiary education and all were in the early stages of study of the same subject. All were in fact required to read textbooks at the same first-year university level, mostly Campbell and Reece (2005). They were of similar ages, although the Swedish subjects were typically a year or so older than the British, and the gender mix (predominantly female) was the same. In both countries some subjects had other home languages and occasionally other L1 languages than English or Swedish (such as Gujerati, Arabic, or Kurdish) although the majority had Swedish (the "L2" group) or English (the "L1" group) as their L1 and as their home language. However, all subjects had taken secondary education in the official local language. This constellation represents typical students in the two communities.

Instruments

When we initially piloted several of our tests, we included the Swedish National Test for comprehension of Swedish texts. Although we had only 15 students in the piloting trials, the reading comprehension product scores for Swedish and English correlated strongly, and those with weak Swedish reading comprehension also showed weak English reading comprehension. It was quite clear that those with weaker comprehension scores were those who did not have Swedish as the L1, making Swedish their L2 and English their L3. Due to the very strong correlation across the Swedish and English comprehension tests, and the pressure of time, the Swedish tests were dropped in our testing of the Swedish students.

Our battery of tests consists of a set of paper-based tests and a set of computer-based tests using the program Superlab (Abboud & Sugar, 1990). The following tests were used for this study. 1–4 are the paper-based tests and 5–6 the Superlab-based tests.

1. *Comprehension test:* a multiple-choice test consisting of ten texts with four questions following each text. The questions types targeted (1) explicitly stated information, (2) paraphrased information, (3) inference information, and (4) summary type information. Subjects were given 25 minutes to complete the test. Instructions for both groups were the same: answer as many questions as best you can within the 25 minute period.

2. *Vocabulary tests:* One section of this test consisted of words from the Academic Word List (Coxhead, 2000) in a fill-in-the-blank style test. The second section consisted of 30 multiple-choice synonym and antonym questions with no context adapted from a collection of college-entrance examination vocabulary learning questions. Subjects were given 20 minutes to complete the test.

3. *Inferencing.* This test, based on Hannon and Daneman (2001), was used to test the higher-order skills of readers without requiring extensive knowledge of the L2. Hannon and Daneman say that their test measures "individual differences in four components of reading comprehension: the ability to access prior knowledge from long-term memory, to integrate accessed prior knowledge with new text information, to make inferences based on information provided in the text, and to recall the new text information from memory"

(p. 105). Thus, it provides a convenient general assessment of a selection of higher-level reading-related skills. It correlates well with direct measures of reading comprehension but, crucially from our point of view, taps only higher-level components and its results are little influenced by specific language knowledge or processing. Basic vocabulary together with non-words are used to elicit true-false responses, as in this example:

A NORT resembles a JET but is faster and weighs more.
A BERL resembles a CAR but is slower and weighs more.
A SAMP resembles a BERL but is slower and weighs more.

1. A JET is faster than a BERL.   T
2. A ROCKET is faster than a BERL.   T
3. Like ROCKETS, BERLS travel in the air.   F

Subjects had 10 minutes to complete the test.

4. *Recall:*   Students were given a text of 800 words about plant hormones called gibberellins taken directly from a comparable biology textbook to what they were using in their courses, complete with accompanying pictures. The students were given 10 minutes to read the text and then, without having the text to refer to, were given 10 minutes to write a summary of the text. The Swedish students were told that they could write their summary in either Swedish or English (see Brantmeier [2006] on answering test questions in the L2). Scores were calculated in several stages. First, the primary text was analyzed and broken down into propositional sized statements, agreed upon by the current authors. Second, each written protocol, after being typed into a file, was analyzed and compared to this "key." For every proposition produced by the subject one point was given (in some instances, half-points). Two external raters practiced rating the summaries until there was fairly good agreement. Finally, all the summaries were scrutinized, scored, and the number of propositions for each summary was tallied. Although the recall-protocols were time-consuming to evaluate, they provided valuable information concerning the range of abilities of the students in text modeling and recall.

5. *Word recognition* (lexical decision).   In this test there were 50 items of 5-letter sequences of possible English words that were presented on the computer screen. Students responded with a Yes (left mouse button) or No (right mouse button). The computer kept track of the answers and the response time for each item. There were 25 words and 25 non-words. The aim was to assess (automatic) word-recognition speed.

6. *Sentence coherence.* In this test there were 50 sentences that were presented on the computer screen one by one. Each sentence consisted of two clauses that were explicitly linked with a subordinating conjunction. The informants were to decide whether the clauses created a coherent sentence. For example, the sentence 'Fish is becoming expensive because the moon orbits the earth' would be incoherent while 'I need to borrow some money because I left my wallet at home' would be coherent. The aim was to test the (controlled) processing speed relating two simple clauses.

To date we have tested a total of 100 Swedish (L2) first year biology students on tests 1–4. Of these we have further tested fifteen Swedish students on the computer-based tests 5 and 6. A total of 49 British ("L1") first year biology students have been given tests 1–4 and 19 have been given the computer-based process tests.

RESULTS

The first step was to divide the subjects into appropriate groups. The mean score of the British subjects on the multiple-choice reading comprehension test was 18.06, with a standard deviation of 4.26. Subjects with scores of 13 and above were within one SD of the mean, and those with scores of 9 or above were within two SDs. Table 7.1 shows how the subjects were divided.

Subjects who scored below 9 were omitted as less proficient than the population of interest. This involved leaving out three British subjects, of whom two were second-language users of English and 22 Swedish. Table 7.1 shows that the majority of the British subjects scored within the range of the "very-advanced" Swedes. This means that this group of Swedes constitute the top three deciles of the volunteers sampled, while the equivalent group of British subjects cover almost nine deciles of the volunteers.

For all tasks described below, the variance among the L2 readers was greater than that for the L1 readers. Some of the L2 readers were even in the high L1 efficiency range (which should justify the category of "native-like" reading proficiency). The overall results of the tests are given in Table 7.2 and the in-

TABLE 7.1 Division of Subjects

Score	L1 group	L2 group
13+	Included ($N = 40$)	"very-advanced" $N = 30$
9–12	Included ($N = 6$)	"less-advanced" $N = 48$
Less than 9	Excluded (3)	Excluded (22)

dividual results for each test are discussed below. Table 7.2 gives the raw scores and standard deviations for the paper tests, but for the computer tests (word recognition and sentence coherence) it gives efficiency scores, which are computed by dividing the mean accuracy score by the mean response time. Only correct answers for real words and for coherent sentences were counted.

The same scores, adjusted so that each test is shown to the same scale for easy comparison, are shown graphically in Figure 7.1. It can be seen

TABLE 7.2 Results of Tasks

	L1	L2-very	L2-less
Comprehension test	17.80	17.67	10.48
	4.26	4.01	1.41
Inferencing	17.42	17.63	15.87
	2.53	2.22	3.65
Recall	12.40	9.33	7.03
	5.10	3.39	2.87
Vocabulary	41.81	30.04	14.54
	11.10	14.39	9.54
Word recognition	27.60	24.09	
	4.26	6.92	
Sentence coherence	5.28	3.83	
	1.40	1.85	

Note: Means are italicized, standard deviations under each mean.

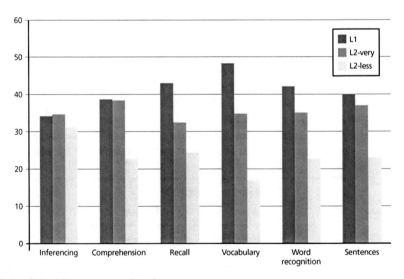

Figure 7.1 Mean scores related to means across groups.

that the inference test is the least discriminatory and the vocabulary test discriminates the most. It can be seen from Table 7.2 and Figure 7.1 that the inferencing scores for the very-advanced group are fully comparable to those of the L1 group. For the word recognition and sentence coherence tests, as well as overall, the advanced L2 group has a mean score closer to the L1 group than it does to the less-advanced group. On the other hand, both L2 groups show weaker recall and vocabulary scores. The more specific results of each test will be discussed in turn.

Inferencing

This task was intended as a fairly pure test of inferencing skill. The aim was to measure inferencing abilities without having vocabulary as a factor, i.e., the vocabulary level was very basic. An additional point is that all the test subjects seemed to have sufficient time to complete the task; there were a few who did not finish the test in the allotted time. Table 7.3 shows that there was a ceiling effect but the very-advanced L2 readers had a mean score comparable to, even marginally higher than, the L1 readers. The less-advanced L2 group had scores significantly below these levels (t-test, $p < .05$ compared with both the very-advanced and the L1 groups).

Comprehension Test

This timed multiple-choice test gave information both on reading speed and on accuracy. The total scores used for assessing comprehension do not differentiate between question types so that students who were more efficient in inferencing and those more efficient in "gistification" (summarizing) are not distinguished at this stage.

This was a rather challenging test and scores out of a possible 40 were quite low, as shown in Table 7.4. The very-advanced L2 users scored almost the same as the L1 users, while the less-advanced l2 readers were (by definition) much lower.

However, Table 7.4 also shows that the completion rates were rather different. Although there was little difference in the total scores of the L1 and very-advanced L2 groups, the L1 readers attempted many more questions

TABLE 7.3   Inferencing Scores

	L1	L2-very	L2-less
Inference test scores	17.42	17.63	15.87

TABLE 7.4   Results of the Multiple-Choice Reading Comprehensions Test

Comprehension test	L1	L2-very	L2-less
Mean score out of 40	17.80	17.67	10.48
Standard deviation	4.26	4.01	1.41
Number of questions attempted	34.38	25.61	20.48

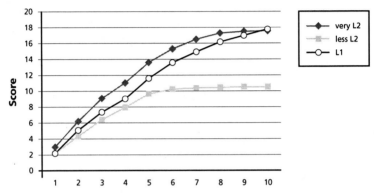

Figure 7.2   Cumulative scores on comprehension test for the British and Swedish groups.

than either L2 group. All subjects attempted the first 16 questions (the first four texts), and Figure 7.2, which shows the cumulative scores achieved at the end of each text, shows that until question 4 the total average scores were rather similar for the less-advanced L2 group and the L1 group. At that point they started to diverge and the L1 group continued to increase cumulative score almost linearly while both L2 groups leveled off, so that the very-advanced L2 readers and the L1 group ended with very similar scores. This indicates that the Swedish groups simply did not have time to complete more.

In view of this finding, the scores for only the first 4 texts were calculated, and the result is shown in Figure 7.3. This gives rather different results, with the L1 group averaging 8.26 correct answers (to 16 questions) and the broad L2 group averaging 8.88. Figure 7.3 shows that the very-advanced L2 group had higher scores on average than the L1 group on the first four questions. This is not surprising since the very-advanced L2 group consists of the top scorers in the broad L2 group while the L1 group had many low scorers.

It is clear from these figures that if one ignores the effect of time constraints the L1 and the L2 groups achieve similar levels of accuracy. Ignoring time constraints the L1 group scores the same as the less-advanced L2

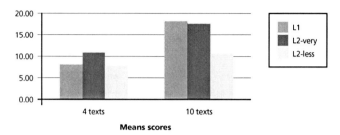

Figure 7.3 Comprehension scores calculated on four and ten texts.

TABLE 7.5   Scores on Inference Questions on the Reading Comprehension Test

	L1	L2-very	L2-less
Inference questions	3.41	3.53	1.52

group, who represent the middle proficiency range of the L2 population sample, and they do not therefore seem to have any accuracy advantage. On the other hand, including time constraints they score the same as the most advanced L2 readers.

One might speculate that the very-advanced L2 readers may have prioritized accuracy over speed, while many of the weaker L1 readers may have done the opposite.

The comprehension test included one question for each text that involved elaborative inferencing. When the scores for only these 10 questions are tallied, the results are comparable to those of the inferencing test. The L1 group had a mean of 3.4, while the broad L2 group had a mean of 2.29, and the very-advanced group had a mean of 3.5 and the less-advanced group 1.5. These scores and the inference test scores are shown in Table 7.5. The very-advanced L2 readers consistently reach L1 levels on inferencing questions while the less-advanced L2 readers are considerably below.

An analysis including time constraints shows a more complex pattern as in Figure 7.4. While the less-advanced L2 group always scored less on inferencing questions than the other two, the very advanced group scored better than the L1 readers on the elaboration-inferencing questions on texts 1, 2, 3, 5, and 7; they scored worse than the L1 group on the relevant questions on texts 4, 6 and 8 and did not attempt questions 9 and 10. There appears to be the same pattern of superior accuracy in the advanced L2 group balanced by slower reading and therefore a similar overall mean score compared to the less accurate but faster natives. The less-advanced L2 readers are both less accurate and slower on inferencing, as their score on the inferencing test suggests.

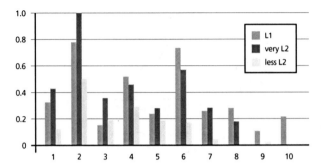

Figure 7.4   Mean score per question for elaboration-inferencing questions.

Recall Task

The scores from the reading comprehension test and the recall task could both be used to rate whole-skill reading comprehension. Both tasks require rather sophisticated text modeling, especially the recall task. As noted above, Swedish subjects were allowed to write their summaries in either Swedish or English, and roughly a third of the subjects used English. The underlying hypothesis behind this task is that to optimize recall of a rather complex text, a reader would need to create a quite sophisticated model (or models) of the text. This model would have stronger links for causally linked factors (e.g., that gibberellins caused dwarf plants to produce normal growth) and temporal links (e.g., when various discoveries related to gibberellins were made) and weaker links to information that was of a more incidental nature.

For this task, the very-advanced L2 readers had mean scores closer to the less-advanced L2 reader than the L1 readers (Table 7.2). This would seem to suggest that the L2 group as a whole is somewhat disadvantaged compared to the L1 group in this complex task involving memorization and production as well as elaboration of a model. Testing the L2 students with more time to read the texts had relatively little effect on the number of propositions they produced.

Vocabulary

The vocabulary test revealed the greatest differences among the groups. The L1 group has of course a much better average knowledge of the vocabulary of their own language than the L2 groups. However it is striking that the large differences in vocabulary knowledge do not correspond to differences in accuracy of reading product in the multiple-choice test, where we saw that the very advanced L2 readers did better than the L1 readers. It would seem that this vocabulary weakness among the L2 readers must be compensated for in some way.

Word Recognition

This test was administered to a subset of subjects. It measured response times to words and non-words as described above. The L2 groups are summed since the number of advanced L2 subjects that performed these two tasks is rather low ($N = 15$). For the word recognition task, only correct answers to real words were counted; for the sentence coherence task described below only response times for correct answers for coherent sentences were included.

The scores given in Table 7.2 above are efficiency scores, i.e., accuracy divided by response time. The accuracy scores (recognition of only real words) alone are somewhat different, as shown in Table 7.6.

Once again the L2 readers as a whole have comparable accuracy scores to the L1 readers, while efficiency is lower because they had longer response times.

Sentence Processing

Like the word recognition scores, the sentence coherence accuracy scores for the L2 group are comparable to the L1 group, as shown in Table 7.7. Only those answers that correspond to coherent sentences were count-

TABLE 7.6   Accuracy and Efficiency Scores for Word Recognition Task

Word recognition	L1	L2
Accuracy	23.26	22.93
Efficiency	27.60	24.09

TABLE 7.7   Accuracy and Efficiency Scores for Sentence Coherence Task

Sentence coherence	L1	L2
Accuracy	16.32	15.67
Efficiency	5.28	3.83

TABLE 7.8 Scores of the Very-Advanced L2 Group as a Proportion of the L1 Group on the One Hand, and of the Less-Advanced L2 Group as a Proportion of the Very-Advanced L2 Group on the Other

	L2-v / L1	L2-l / L2-v
Comprehension	97.8	59.3
Inferencing	101.2	90.0
Recall	75.2	75.3
Vocabulary	71.8	48.4
Word recognition	87.3	
Sentence coherence	72.5	

ed. Although the accuracy of the very-advanced L2 group is as high as that of the L1 students, the difference in efficiency is due to the L2s' generally slower reaction times.

Table 7.8 gives an overview of the relative performance levels of the two L2 groups, i.e., where they have their strengths and weaknesses. The first column of figures gives the accuracy scores of the very-advanced L2 group as a percentage of the corresponding scores of the L1 group, while the second column gives corresponding scores for the less-advanced L2 group as a percentage of those of the very-advanced group. Clearly, both L2 groups scored well on the inferencing test, although only the very-advanced group also scored high on the inferencing questions on the comprehension test (see Table 7.4 above). The areas in which the differences between the L2 groups and the L1 readers were greatest were recall—the most demanding task—and vocabulary—the most purely "linguistic" test.

DISCUSSION

In summary, a multiple choice format reading comprehension test was used to separate the advanced L2 readers into two groups: the very-advanced L2 group that had scores above 1 standard deviation below the L1 mean, and the less-advanced L2 group that had scores on this test between 1 and 2 standard deviations below the L1 mean. With this arbitrary division, a number of additional tasks were performed by these two groups as well as by a British counterpart group (first year biology students).

One expectation from the literature was that the relevant differences between the mean performances of L1 and advanced L2 readers would primarily be due to linguistic factors, and, consequently, that only weak word processing, from the list of potential problem areas given by McNamara, de

Vega, and O'Reilly (2007) discussed above, would apply to both poor L1 readers and advanced L2 readers. In practice, however, the less-advanced L2 group scored significantly below the others on the inference test, although there seemed to be a ceiling effect for this task. The significance of this is discussed below.

On the other tasks (recall, vocabulary, word recognition, and sentence coherence recognition) the less-advanced L2 group scored markedly below the L1 group and the very-advanced L2 group (see Figure 7.1 above). Particularly noticeable was the difference on the vocabulary test where the very-advanced L2 group had a mean score of 72% of the mean L1 score and the less-advanced L2 group had a mean score of 48% of the very-advanced L2 mean (and 35% of the L1 mean). It should be recalled that the very-advanced L2 group consisted of the best scorers in the L2 group, while the mean L1 score was based on a broad range of L1 reading skills among the tested biology students.

Several researchers have claimed (McNamara & O'Reilly, 2007; Long et al., 2006) that vocabulary knowledge and word recognition skills are weaker in poor L1 readers than in good L1 readers. We also find weaker vocabulary knowledge and slower word-identification skills in the L2 groups generally. The very-advanced L2 group seems able to compensate for these weaknesses by relying on inferencing skills as proposed by Bernhardt (2005), but the less-advanced group seems to be inhibited in higher-level skills by linguistic disadvantage.

We might describe our very advanced L2 reader as a very skilled inferencer who compares well with L1 counterparts on whole-skill reading comprehension if given sufficient time. While somewhat disadvantaged in speed, these readers seem to perform well in terms of accuracy. Further improvement in L2 reading for such readers would seem to be primarily a question of automatization (word recognition) and increased vocabulary knowledge.

Even the less-advanced L2 readers demonstrate fairly good inferencing skills, but they seem less able to make use of these skills in tasks under time pressure. Their scores for all tasks are below those of the very-advanced L2 readers. We know from the pilot tests that they represent an average group of readers in their own language, and that therefore the differences from the scores of the L1 group, who are also a cross-section, are due to the language difference. Their higher-level skills are not outstanding and one could speculate that the processing demands of lower level skills such as word recognition and accessing vocabulary information drain resources that could be used for higher level inferencing. The fact that these readers score relatively better on the inferencing task, but relatively worse on the comprehension questions that require some degree of elaborative inferencing from given textual information, suggests that competing processes might be sapping resources otherwise used in on-line inferencing.

In contrast, the very-advanced L2 readers performed at or above L1 accuracy means for comprehension questions requiring elaborative inferencing. The less-advanced L2 readers appear disadvantaged because their L2 knowledge is weaker, which slows down the reading and comprehension processing generally. Under time pressure, this handicap draws resources away from what would otherwise be a strength, that is general inferencing. It would seem then, that a high level of L2 knowledge is required before the inferencing skills begin to be fully effective as compensatory skills, at least for tasks that put performance pressure on the reader. The question, then, is whether this 'threshold' of advanced L2 knowledge and skills can be described and measured so that the very large group of less-advanced L2 readers can be enabled to compete on more equal terms with L1 counterparts.

From the results of the various tests given to the L1 and advanced L2 readers, several generalizations can be proposed. First of all, unlike poor L1 readers, it seems that neither group of L2 readers had problems with inferencing (McNamara & O'Reilly, 2006; Long et al., 2006).

Although our inferencing test primarily captured relational inferences, the kind of inferencing we assume is an asset for the advanced L2 reader would include general cultural background knowledge, bridging inferencing skill, perhaps even elaborative inferencing skill. Although the tasks underpinning this study do not cover all sub-skills of reading, we would like to suggest that the advanced L2 readers as a group make use of general inferencing skill to compensate for weaker lower-level processing skills such as vocabulary knowledge and word recognition skill. The L2 readers generally have much weaker vocabularies (vocabulary size, vocabulary depth was not tested) than the L1 readers, at least in the academic and low-frequency range of English vocabulary. Clahsen and Felser (2006) suggest that adult L2 users make greater use of semantic cues than syntactic ones in decoding texts ('shallow syntax'). While semantic processing is usually considered distinct from inferencing skills, neither skill is directly tied to explicit textual markers (whether lexical or syntactic).

Second, the overall result that the advanced L2 readers are accurate but slower suggests that perhaps the L2 readers have less automated lower-level processing and are compensating by relying on higher-level processes, such as inferencing.

Segalowitz and Hulstijn (2005) propose a calculation for comparing processing speeds among different readers or populations of readers. The underlying idea is that as processing becomes automated, the ratio of mean processing time to standard deviation will increase. Merely speeding up a process would not produce a smaller standard deviation whereas a truly automated process would, according to Segalowitz and Hulstijn. The response time figures for the two computer-based tasks, the word recognition task and the sentence coherence task, can be used to view the extent to which the L2 groups have automated their L2 reading processing. In Tables 7.9 and 7.10, a comparison of the response time means and standard deviations are shown for the word recognition task and the sentence coherence task.

For the word recognition task we see that the coefficient of variation is substantially greater for the L1 group, which indicates that the L1 subjects have more automated word recognition processing than do the L2 subjects. The difference between the coefficients of variation for the sentence coherence task, on the other hand, is not as great.

We propose that the task itself relies to a greater extent on controlled processing. As described above, many of the sentences used in this task were reversals of normal expectations. In a sentence such as *The couple decide to buy the house although it was quite inexpensive*, the concessive subordinator would normally be used to indicate an obstacle of some kind, such as a high price. We would speculate that the L1 users were compelled to slow down and consciously interpret the sense of such sentences. As a consequence, they approached all the sentences in the same, controlled manner, not knowing beforehand which were reversals and which were not. Consequently, what Table 7.9 tells us is that this task involved more controlled processing than the word recognition task and that less difference in the coefficient of variation is the expected result.

Third, we have a generalization about compensatory processes. Walczyk (2000, p. 563) points out that the magnitude of correlations between processing (verbal) efficiency and comprehension product among L1 read-

TABLE 7.9 Coefficient of Variation for Word Recognition Task

	Accuracy Means	Response time Means	Response time SDs	Coeff. of variation
L1 group	23.26	863	313	2.76
L2 group	22.93	1036	555	1.87

TABLE 7.10 Coefficient of Variation for Sentence Coherence Task

	Accuracy Means	Response time Means	Response time SDs	Coeff. of variation
L1 group	16.32	3308	1190	2.78
L2 group	15.67	4730	2076	2.28

ers will be greatest when reading occurs in situations where there is severe time pressure, as in many test situations. The reason is that readers have less opportunity to slow down, reread, look back, and so on when reading under pressure, so that those with low verbal efficiency will also have a low comprehension score. In circumstances with little pressure low-efficiency readers can make use of various compensating behaviors and strategies.

It would seem that something similar is taking place with the less-advanced L2 readers. While the very-advanced L2 readers seem able to make use of inferencing skills to compensate for less-automated lower-level processing, the less-advanced L2 readers do not seem able to utilize this means of compensatory processing.

It should be mentioned that our results were not in complete agreement with those of the van Gelderen et al. (2004) study mentioned above, where low-level processing (e.g., word recognition) correlates quite highly with comprehension test scores. In our studies a multiple-choice comprehension test was used as the instrument for distinguishing the very-advanced from the less-advanced. The results of the other tests vary by task, but we generally did not find the same level of correlation that van Gelderen et al. found.

One explanation for the difference may be the fact that our informants were somewhat more sophisticated readers than the secondary school students used in the van Gelderen et al. study, and to a greater extent may have developed various compensating strategies for less effective reading components. An additional explanatory factor is background knowledge as a compensatory resource. It seems reasonable to assume that there is greater variation in general and topic specific background knowledge among university students than among upper secondary school students. This greater variation may reduce correlations between comprehension scores, where compensatory resources can be utilized, and lower-level processes such as word-recognition.

Concerning our first research question, the variance in product scores among the various groups depends on the task and the criterion. However, the less-advanced L2 group achieved lower scores than the L1 group did on all tasks, whatever the criteria. The pattern between the very-advanced L2 group and the L1 group is more complex, with the very-advanced L2 group having an accuracy advantage where time is not an issue, and an advantage in inferencing tasks, but the L1 group reads faster and does better on the most complex task, the recall task.

This means that the answer to the second question is that the L1 readers are substantially faster even than the very-advanced L2 readers, which in turn means that their efficiency scores are higher, even though the very-advanced L2 group shows signs of better comprehension quality and more sophisticated inferencing.

To answer the third question, it seems that the main difference between the very-advanced L2 readers and the less-advanced L2 readers is in reading quality. The very-advanced are indeed somewhat faster, but they are also much better at getting the gist, inferencing, and they have much larger vocabularies.

While the results of this study indicate that the advanced L2 population consists of a range of L2 reading proficiencies, the tasks discussed above suggest that many supposedly advanced L2 readers are clearly disadvantaged in relation to L1 counterparts reading the same textbooks. Nonetheless, there is a minority of advanced L2 readers who attain accuracy scores fully comparable to those of counterpart L1 readers, although it takes them longer. Additional study is necessary to better describe the relationship between low-level processing, primarily word recognition and vocabulary knowledge, and higher-level comprehension processes. In the meantime, it would seem that for the majority of L2 readers of English textbooks at university, improving vocabulary skills might be a path toward greater comprehension of L2 texts.

ACKNOWLEDGMENTS

This project is part of the AAA programme at Stockholm University. We would like to thank the Swedish Riksbankens Jubileumsfond for funding this project, and Ann-Kristin Östlund-Farrants, Aileen Irving, and Michael Shaw for their help.

REFERENCES

Abboud, H., & Sugar, D. (1990). *Superlab Pro: Experimental laboratory software*. Phoenix: Cedrus Corp.

Bernhardt, E. (2005). Progress and procrastination in second language reading. *Annual Review of Applied Linguistics, 25*, 133–150.

Brantmeier, C. (2006). The effects of language of assessment and L2 reading performance on advanced readers' recall. *The Reading Matrix, 6*(1), 1–17.

Campbell, N A., & Reece, J. B. (2005). *Biology*. New York: Prentice-Hall.

Clahsen, H., & Felser, C. (2006). Grammatical processing in first and second language learners. *Applied Psycholinguistics, 27*, 3–42.

Coxhead A. (2000). A new academic word list. *TESOL quarterly, 34*(2) 213–238.

Fukkink, R. G., Hulstijn, J., & Simis, A. (2005). Does training in second-language word recognition skills affect reading comprehension? An experimental study. *The Modern Language Journal, 89*(1), 54–75.

Gernsbacher, M. A., & St. John, M. F. (2001). Modeling suppression in lexical access. In D. Gorfein (Ed.), *On the consequences of meaning* (pp. 119–132). Washington, DC: APA Publications.

Graddol, D. (2006). *English Next.* London: British Council.

Hannon, B., & Daneman, M. (2001). A new tool for measuring and understanding individual differences in the component processes of reading comprehension. *Journal of Educational Psychology, 93*(1), 103–128.

Hyltenstam, K. (1988). Lexical characteristics of near-native second-language learners of Swedish. *Journal of Multilingual and Multicultural Development, 9*(1–2), 67–84.

Koda, K. (2004). *Insights into second language reading: A cross-linguistic approach.* Cambridge: Cambridge University Press.

Long, D. L., Johns, C. L., & Morris, P. E. (2006). Comprehension ability in mature readers. In M. Traxler & M. Gernsbacher (Eds.), *Handbook of psycholinguistics* (2nd ed., pp. 801–833). Amsterdam: Elsevier.

McNamara, D. S., de Vega, M., & O'Reilly, T. (2007). Comprehension skill, inference making, and the role of knowledge. In F. Schmalhofer & C. Perfetti (Eds.), *Higher level language processes in the brain: Inference and comprehension processes* (pp. 233–251). Mahwah, NJ: Lawrence Erlbaum.

Segalowitz, N. S., & Hulstijn, J. (2005). Automaticity in bilingualism and second language learning. In J. Kroll & A. M. B. de Groot (Eds.), *Handbook of bilingualism, psycholinguistic approaches* (pp. 371–388). Oxford: Oxford University Press.

Shaw, P., & McMillion, A. (2008). Proficiency effects and compensation in advanced second-language reading. *Nordic Journal of English Studies, 7*(3), 124–144.

Snellings, P., van Gelderen, A., & de Glopper, K. (2002). Lexical retrieval: An aspect of fluent second language production that can be enhanced. *Language Learning, 52*(4), 723–754.

van den Broek, P., Risden, K., & Husebye-Hartmann, E. (1995). The role of readers' standards of coherence in the generation of inferences during reading. In R. F. Lorch, Jr. & E. J. O'Brien (Eds.), *Sources of coherence in reading* (pp. 353–373). Hillsdale, NJ: Lawrence Erlbaum.

van den Broek, P., Virtue, S., Everson, M., Tzeng, Y., & Sung, Y. (2002). Comprehension and memory of science texts: Inferential processes and the construction of a mental representation. In J. Otero (Ed.), *Psychology of science text comprehension* (pp. 131–154). Mahwah, NJ: Lawrence Erlbaum.

van Gelderen, A., Schoonen, R., de Glopper, K., Hulstijn, J., Simil, A., Snellings, P., & Stevenson, M. (2004). Linguistic knowledge, processing speed, and metacognitive knowledge in first- and second-language reading comprehension: A componential analysis. *Journal of Educational Psychology, 96*(1), 19–30.

Walczyk, J. J. (2000). The interplay between automatic and control processes in reading. *Reading Research Quarterly, 35*(4), 554–566.

Walter, C. (2007). First- to second-language reading comprehension: not transfer, but access. *International Journal of Applied Linguistics, 17*(1), 14–37.

Zwaan, R. A., & Radvansky, G. A. (1998). Situation models in language comprehension and memory. *Psychological Bulletin, 123*, 162–185.

CHAPTER 8

GENDER AND FOREIGN LANGUAGE READING COMPREHENSION

The Effects of Strategy Training

Jeanne M. Schueller

ABSTRACT

Over the past few decades, the study of learner variables in foreign- and second-language learning has emerged as a way to investigate how and why language learners vary in their acquisition of the target language. Results from such studies point toward several individual factors that play a role in foreign-language (FL) learning, including age, aptitude, motivation, learning strategies, learning styles, anxiety, personality, and gender. The interaction between gender and FL reading comprehension has received more interest recently as researchers have examined the relationship between gender and various nonlinguistic factors. The present study examines the effects of strategic training on reading comprehension by gender. More specifically, it analyzes the efficacy of pre-reading strategy training in either conceptually driven top-down strategies or text-bound bottom-up strategies. Results show that subjects in the top-down treatment group outperform subjects who re-

Crossing Languages and Research Methods, pages 147–167
Copyright © 2009 by Information Age Publishing
All rights of reproduction in any form reserved.

ceived bottom-up or no training, that females outperform males on nearly all assessment measures, and that males were less homogeneous as a group than were the females.

INTRODUCTION

Over the past few decades, the study of learner variables in foreign- and second-language learning has emerged as a way to investigate how and why language learners vary in their acquisition of the target language (TL).[1] Results from such studies point toward several individual factors that play a role in foreign- and second-language learning, including age, aptitude, motivation, learning strategies, learning styles, anxiety, personality, and gender. While studies have shown that reading comprehension is significantly affected by appropriate strategy use and awareness of strategy use, little research has examined the role of gender as a learner variable in foreign-language (FL) reading comprehension. The interaction between gender and FL reading comprehension has received more interest of late as researchers have examined the relationship between gender and nonlinguistic factors such as strategy use, topic familiarity, proficiency, and enjoyment. The present study combines two strands of research on learner variables, strategy use, and gender to examine the effects of strategic training on reading comprehension by gender. These issues are of particular interest to FL instructors who are limited in the type and amount of pre-reading activities they can feasibly include in their lessons due to time constraints and who lack compelling evidence by which to judge the efficacy of different types of pre-reading activities.

FL READING COMPREHENSION

FL reading comprehension results from a complex interaction of text-based and conceptual strategies. Previous research has revealed a variety of strategies believed to be employed by successful readers, including retaining meaning in short-term memory, skipping unfamiliar words, relying on the context and real-world knowledge, and identifying the grammatical category of words (Hosenfeld et al., 1981 in Schulz, 1983, p. 129). Furthermore, a successful reader must be able to employ multiple strategies depending on the text and the task. TOP-DOWN strategies mark higher-level, conceptually driven processing in which readers rely on their background knowledge to make and test hypotheses about the text, thereby facilitating global or synthetic comprehension. Examples of top-down reading strategies include, for example, having expectations and making predictions about the text, brainstorming the topic, semantic mapping, triggering background knowledge, skimming the text for its gist, considering the genre and discourse structure, finding out background information about the author, making inferences, identifying main points, and summarizing while reading. BOTTOM-UP strategies, on the other hand, reflect lower-level linguistic processing and include analytical or detail-oriented strategies that aid the reader in problem-solving, such as attention to linguistic competence (targeting specific vocabulary or grammatical structures), decoding meaning, using cognates, scanning the text for details, using a dictionary or glossary, and translating from the L1 into the L2. An overview of top-down and bottom-up strategies can be found in Table 8.1.[2]

FL learners face certain obstacles while reading in the TL that may not be problematic when reading in the native language (NL). For example, FL readers possess *limited* lexical knowledge, knowledge of the linguistic code, and cultural and pragmatic knowledge, but *increased* attention to lower-level processing and failure to activate schemata. Proficiency seems to be strongly associated with the reading process and constitutes a fundamental difference between L1 and L2 reading, whereby L1 readers focus more on higher-level processing, while L2 readers are more likely to engage in lower-level processing (Carrell, 1989; Horiba, 1996). Kern (1989) found that L2 readers are more linguistically bound to the text than are L1 readers. Furthermore, because L1 readers are less burdened by linguistic elements of the text, they have readier access to background knowledge and schemata that foster global reading comprehension. Carrell (1989, p. 127) finds

TABLE 8.1 Overview of Top-Down and Bottom-Up Reading Strategies

Top-Down (global, synthetic, "big-picture-oriented" strategies)	Bottom-Up (local, analytical, "detail-oriented" strategies)
• focusing on the "big picture"	• focusing on details
• using background knowledge and knowledge of the world	• bound to information in the text
• Brainstorming	• focusing on linguistic elements and grammatical features
• skimming for an overview or gist	• scanning for specific information
• hypothesizing & testing predictions	• morphologically, syntactically, phonetically dissecting a word or phrase
• guessing meaning from the context	• decoding meaning via:
• integrating new information with old	– dictionary use
• considering information about the author, year, text genre	– L1 cognates – grammatical category
• summarizing while reading	• translating from the L1 to the L2

that for "reading in the L1, 'local' reading strategies (focusing on grammatical structures, sound-letter correspondences, word-meaning, and text detail) tended to be negatively correlated with reading performance." On the other hand, for higher proficiency L2 readers, "global" reading strategies ("those having to so with background knowledge, text gist, and textual organization") were positively correlated with reading performance (Carrell, 1989, p. 126). Similar results were found by Young (1993) in her study comparing cognitive and affective responses to authentic and edited texts by L2 learners. Young's data indicate that the "successful readers used more global strategies than the less successful readers to process the authentic text" and that successful readers used more global strategies to process the edited text as well (1993, p. 458).

GENDER AND STRATEGY USE

Similar to the findings on successful FL reading comprehension, research strategy on use and learning has shown that in comparison with the behaviors of less successful FL learners, successful FL learners report using strategies more frequently, are more aware of the particular strategies they use, are more likely to select task-appropriate strategies, and are better able to apply strategies efficiently according to task demands (e.g., Barnett, 1988; Carrell, 1989; Green & Oxford, 1995; MacIntyre & Noels, 1996). In fact, learners vary in their strategy use depending on several factors, including gender (e.g., Bacon, 1992; Bacon & Finnemann, 1992; Chavez, 2001; Green & Oxford, 1995; Oxford & Nyikos, 1989).

Indeed, research has revealed gender differences in learning styles and preferences (e.g., Oxford, 1993; Schmeck, 1983): Females are more frequently associated with top-down, males with bottom-up behavior. According to self-report studies investigating the use of language learning strategies, when compared to males, females report greater use of top-down strategies than males and less frequent use of bottom-up strategies (Bacon, 1992; Bacon & Finnemann, 1992; Young & Oxford, 1997).[3] Bacon's (1992) self-report study found no significant differences in listening comprehension between males and females after subjects listened to authentic texts. She did find, however, that males reported using more bottom-up strategies than did females. In addition, females tend to report using strategies more frequently and a greater variety of strategies than do males (Ehrmann & Oxford, 1989; Green & Oxford, 1995).

Young and Oxford (1997) investigated the strategies used by FL learners of Spanish while reading texts in both their NL (English, in this case) and the TL. They were interested in whether males and females would differ in their strategy use as reported in think-aloud, recall protocol scores, and in their levels of understanding and topic familiarity. Results indicate that subjects employed more strategies to process the FL text than the NL text, and that bottom-up strategies were used more when subjects read the FL text. There were no significant differences in the mean use of either top-down or bottom-up strategies by gender, though females did tend to use top-down strategies somewhat more than did males.

Self-report instruments such as the Strategic Inventory for Language Learning (SILL) have been employed in several studies worldwide, with high reliability. However, the accuracy with which subjects are able to report on their own strategy use is unclear, and it is unknown whether the capacity to reliably determine one's strategy use varies by gender. Treatment studies offer another possibility for studying potential gender differences in strategy use. Previous research has supported the benefits of reading strategy training (e.g., Barnett, 1988; Kern, 1989; Kim, 1995; Taglieber et al., 1988). The effects of gender, however, were not measured in those studies. Thus, one question that remains unanswered is how (or whether) males' and females' reading comprehension is affected by pre-reading strategy training. If males and females vary in their reported strategy use, will they also vary in their benefit from different types of strategy training?

RESEARCH QUESTIONS

The present study addresses this issue by considering three research questions:

1. Do males and females benefit similarly in different types of pre-reading stratgy/training, namely, in top-down and bottom-up strategies?
2. Does the level of reading proficiency mediate the efficacy of training in either type of strategy?
3. Do differences in strategic benefits linked to gender vary by proficiency level?

METHODS

Participants

A total of 140 second-year students of German at the university level participated in the study. Data from 12 subjects were discarded because these subjects had indicated prior familiarity with the text *Das Brot* or had not participated in a pretest of reading comprehension, leaving 128 participants. Subjects were assigned to a particular experimental or control group in an effort to regulate group composition by gender.[4] Subjects did not know whether, or how, their group differed from the other groups. Participation was voluntary and anonymous. Course instructors offered some extra credit for participants; the type and amount of extra credit were left up to each instructor.

As proficiency was one of the variables in the present study, subjects completed a pretest of reading comprehension, consisting of three reading passages and 11 corresponding multiple-choice questions, a few weeks prior to the experimental testing period. All passages and multiple-choice items had been pilot tested to ensure that there was no inherent gender bias. The pretest results were used to divide subjects into three levels of proficiency (high, mid, and low) according to natural score breaks.

The experimental design compared treatment, gender, and proficiency within and across experimental groups. The two independent variables were treatment (pre-reading training in top-down or bottom-up strategies) and gender. The dependent variable was reading comprehension, which was measured by the guided-recall protocol and the multiple-choice test. Group composition by treatment, gender, and proficiency level is shown in Table 8.2.

Reading Text

One short, authentic, literary text, *Das Brot* (*The Bread*), by Wolfgang Borchert, was chosen for this study. In light of research (e.g., Brantmeier, 2001, 2003a; Bügel & Buunk, 1996) that suggests that familiarity with the text topic may result in significant differences in reading comprehension by gender, the selected text underwent extensive pretesting that indicated that it and accompanying multiple-choice items were relatively free of gender bias.

TABLE 8.2   Group Composition

	Proficiency levels	Female	Male	Procedure
G_1 ($n = 44$)	high:	6	3	T_1, X, T_2
top-down	mid/low:	24	11	
G_2 ($n = 41$)	high:	4	4	T_1, X, T_2
bottom-up	mid/low:	20	13	
G_3 ($n = 43$)	high:	12	2	T_1, T_2
control	mid/low:	12	17	

Notes: T_1 = pre-test of reading proficiency; T_2 = post-test; X = treatment.

Training Sessions

Training sessions were conducted by the researcher over a period of about ten days during the third and fourth weeks of the semester. Approximately one-third of the subjects received pre-reading training in top-down strategies, a third in bottom-up, and a third served as the control group and received no pre-reading training. In this study, subjects' pre-reading instruction consisted of one treatment comprising several different activities depending on experimental group prior to the subjects' reading the text. All activities were conducted in the TL, though in order to lower anxiety, subjects were permitted to respond in English if they preferred. Pre-reading activities were designed by the researcher to incorporate specific types of strategies, keeping in mind the processing goals of each treatment. That is, the top-down pre-reading activities were intended to activate the learners' schemata and trigger background knowledge and personal experiences relating to the text. The bottom-up pre-reading activities, on the other hand, needed to emphasize focusing on linguistic elements of the text while reading. For the three pre-reading activities, subjects brainstormed background knowledge about the time period during which the story took place (implicitly, World War II); discussed the notion of sacrifice, which is an essential element of the story; and made lists of obstacles potentially faced by people who lived in an unnamed, war-ravaged Central European country during that time. Finally, subjects completed a role play of an exchange based on one that occurs in the text between the two main characters.[5]

The four activities included in the bottom-up treatment sessions were intended to aid subjects with particular linguistic difficulties that they might encounter while reading the text. Verbs were chosen as the main focus because the text, *Das Brot*, is written in the simple past (preterit) tense. Many verbs in German have an irregular preterit, often with a stem vowel change. This can be confusing to L2 readers who no longer recognize the verb from its infinitive form and therefore do not know its meaning. The exercises focused on the meanings and forms of verbs, and on selected nouns thought to be unfamiliar to the subjects. In the pre-reading activities, subjects did four things. First, they matched columns of verbs in the past tense with their infinitives and discussed the meanings of the verbs. Second, they matched sentences using the same verbs in the past tense with paraphrased sentences in the present tense. Third, they worked with word fields to decide which words out of a list were semantically linked.[6] And fourth, they completed a fill-in-the-blank activity incorporating words from the earlier exercises.

Reading Comprehension Assessment Tasks

Subjects completed two comprehension assessment tasks, a guided-recall protocol, and a short multiple-choice test after reading the text. The participants were told they would have to surrender the text before beginning the assessment activities, but they were given ample time to read and reread the text. The recall task preceded the multiple-choice task so that multiple-choice items did not influence the subjects' recall of the text. In an immediate-recall protocol task, readers are free to write about anything they remember from the text and in any order. To facilitate more systematic comparisons across treatment groups, the guided-recall protocol task employed in the present study prompted subjects to describe elements of the text, including the characters, the setting, the actions in sequence, and the motivations (i.e., what led the characters to act in the way they did). The subjects completed the recall protocol in the NL, as research has shown that significantly more of a passage is recalled when subjects are allowed to write in their NL as opposed to in the TL (see Lee, 1986). Following Carrell (1991), the five multiple-choice items were posed in the language of the text and were written in such a way as to safeguard against the readers' ability to choose the correct answer without having understood the content of the text (see Appendix for multiple-choice questions). Subjects had no access to the text while completing the multiple-choice task, so there was no risk of subjects' simply comparing the multiple-choice items with passages in the text to identify the correct answer.

DATA ANALYSIS

The multiple-choice Scantron data were scored and tabulated for each subject by the university testing center. The recall data were scored using an approach that combines previous methods following Bernhardt (1983), who awarded points for "meaningful phrases," and Block (1986), who looked for thesis statements, main ideas, and details, instead of, for example, counting propositions or idea units (see Barnett, 1988; Horiba, 1996; Lee, 1986).

Since the study's main research question sought to identify differences between groups receiving pre-reading training in top-down (gist-oriented) or bottom-up (detail-oriented) strategies, it was important to be able to distinguish between main ideas (gist), supporting ideas (details), and inferential knowledge. To that end, each element of the text was categorized as either a main or a secondary idea. Main ideas included those that were essential to understanding the story or constituted the basic flow of the story; secondary ideas contained elaborative or descriptive details. Both main and secondary ideas were further identified as factual or inferred knowledge

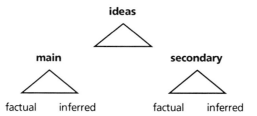

Figure 8.1 Distinction between types and ideas.

(see Figure 8.1). Each idea was assigned a score of one. The maximum number of units was as follows: factual main ideas 39, inferred main ideas 13, factual secondary ideas 63, and inferred secondary ideas 1—resulting in a total of 116 possible elements. Each recall was scored independently by the researcher and by two additional raters. A correlation coefficient of 0.992 suggests strong interrater reliability.

Data were subjected to repeated measures of analysis of variance (ANOVA) and analysis of covariance (ANCOVA) in order to examine the effect of the treatment or control condition on reading comprehension. Fisher's LSD method of multiple comparisons was used to test pairwise comparisons. Independent variables were gender and treatment; proficiency was treated as a covariate. The dependent variable was comprehension as assessed by the recall protocol and the multiple-choice test. Statistical analyses were conducted using two proficiency levels: high and a combined mid/low. Since subjects were divided by proficiency level and gender, many of the groupings had too few subjects to perform statistical tests; therefore, it was necessary to collapse the three proficiency levels into two. ANOVA tests of the pretest scores indicated significant difference between the high and mid proficiency levels, but no significant difference between the mid and low levels. The alpha (or significance) level was set at 0.05.

RESULTS

Overview

Looking first at the recall protocol, statistically significant effects were found for gender (total recall, main, and secondary ideas), the covariate proficiency (total recall and main ideas, near significance [$p < .08$] for inferred ideas), and treatment (inferred ideas), but not for the interaction of treatment and gender. Analyses of the multiple-choice data showed statistical significance for proficiency and treatment, near significance for the interaction of treatment by gender, but none for gender as a main effect. Table 8.3 summarizes the recall protocol and multiple-choice results.

TABLE 8.3 Summary of Recall Protocol and Multiple-Choice Results

	Proficiency	Gender	Treatment	Treatment × gender
Recall Protocol				
Total recall	SIG (p = .024)	SIG (p = .024)	—	—
Main ideas	SIG (p = .021)	SIG (p = .025)	—	—
Secondary ideas	—	SIG (p = .027)	—	—
Inferred ideas	—	—	SIG (p = .003)	—
Multiple Choice	SIG (p = .019)	—	SIG (p = .045)	—

Notes: SIG = significant ($p < .05$); — = not significant

Gender

Gender was a predictor of score for both the recall protocol and the multiple-choice data. Table 8.4 summarizes the results of analyses of the recall protocol data by gender; Table 8.5 lists the means and standard deviations

TABLE 8.4 Recall Protocol Results by Gender

	Total recall		Main ideas		Secondary ideas		Inferred ideas	
	F	M	F	M	F	M	F	M
Proficiency	SIG (p = .023)	—	SIG (p = .027)	—	—	—	—	—
Treatment	—	—	—	—	—	—	SIG (p = .038)	SIG (p = .028)

TABLE 8.5 Recall Protocol Results by Gender

	Total recall		Main ideas		Secondary ideas		Inferred ideas	
	Mean	SD	Mean	SD	Mean	SD	Mean	SD
All females	15.28	0.86	8.70	0.47	4.88	0.36	1.70	0.17
Top-down	16.34	1.38	8.78	0.70	5.30	0.58	2.26	0.28
Bottom-up	15.34	1.53	8.96	0.84	4.57	0.65	1.80	0.31
Control	14.16	1.61	8.35	0.88	4.66	0.68	1.04	0.33
All males	12.09	0.86	6.95	0.60	3.56	0.46	1.59	0.22
Top-down	14.10	2.03	7.87	1.12	3.79	0.86	2.43	0.41
Bottom-up	9.78	1.90	5.75	1.04	2.91	0.80	1.08	0.39
Control	12.44	1.74	7.21	0.96	3.97	0.74	1.26	0.35

of recall protocol scores by treatment and gender. Females' scores showed statistically significant differences by proficiency for total recall, main ideas, and by treatment for inferred ideas; females in the top-down group scored significantly higher than females in the two other experimental groups. Similar to females, males' scores on the recall protocol data showed statistically significant differences by treatment for inferred ideas only, with the males in the top-down group outscoring the males in the other two groups.

Figures 8.2, 8.3, 8.4, and 8.5 juxtapose the mean recall protocol scores for males and females divided by treatment and it appeared that females outperformed males in all areas, though not to statistical significance. Females in the top-down treatment group had the highest mean total recall

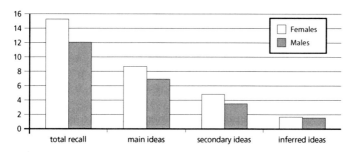

Figure 8.2 Mean recall protocol scores by gender.

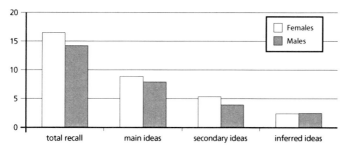

Figure 8.3 Mean recall protocol scores by treatment and gender: Top-down.

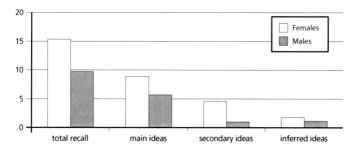

Figure 8.4 Mean recall protocol scores by treatment and gender: Bottom-up.

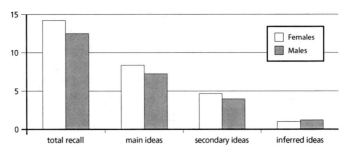

Figure 8.5   Mean recall protocol scores by treatment and gender: Control.

protocol scores, followed by females in the bottom-up group and then females in the control group. Males in the top-down group outscored males
in the two other groups, and males in the control group had a higher score
than did males in the bottom-up treatment group.

None of the analyses of the multiple-choice data was significant for females; however, the males' scores revealed significant differences between
treatment groups: The males in the top-down treatment group achieved
the highest mean scores of the three experimental groups, followed by the
control group, and lastly, the bottom-up treatment group. The difference
between the males' scores in the top-down and bottom-up groups was statistically significant. In fact, the males in the top-down group had the highest
mean score on the multiple-choice items of all six groups (three treatment
groups for males and females). Figure 8.6 shows the mean multiple-choice
scores by treatment and gender.

Proficiency

Of the 128 subjects, 97 were categorized as mid/low-baseline proficient; the remaining 31 were considered to have high-baseline proficiency. Proficiency was analyzed in four subsets: (1) mid/low proficiency, (2)
high proficiency, (3) mid/low females, and (4) mid/low males. The subset containing high-proficiency females or males were too small to analyze
for statistical significance. The recall protocol data yielded statistically significant differences for total recall and main ideas. Only one of the four
groupings described above showed a significant treatment effect. Within
each level of proficiency, no statistically significant differences in total
scores were found among experimental groups; however, among the high
proficiency subjects, the top-down treatment group produced significantly more inferred ideas (3.67) than the high proficiency subjects in the

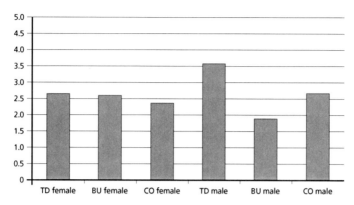

Figure 8.6 Mean multiple-choice scores by treatment and gender.

TABLE 8.6 Recall Protocol Scores by Proficiency Group

		Top-Down		Bottom-Up		Control	
		Mean	**SD**	**Mean**	**SD**	**Mean**	**SD**
Total recall	Mid/low	14.257	1.282	13.09	1.32	12.45	1.41
	High	20.444	2.685	11.63	2.85	16.71	2.15
Main ideas	Mid/low	7.57	0.682	7.82	0.70	7.38	0.74
	High	11.778	1.586	6.25	1.68	9.57	1.27
Secondary ideas	Mid/low	4.74	0.548	3.82	0.57	3.86	0.60
	High	5.00	1.094	3.88	1.16	5.93	0.88
Inferred ideas	Mid/low	1.94	0.260	1.46	0.27	1.21	0.29
	High	3.67*	0.505	1.50	0.54	1.21	0.41

two other experimental groups (Bottom-up: 1.50; Control: 1.21; $p = .002$). Table 8.6 lists the means and standard deviations of recall protocol scores divided by proficiency groups.

Baseline proficiency was significant for the multiple-choice data between the two treatment groups and the control group, but treatment group as a main effect was not significant within the proficiency subset groups. Among the three experimental groups, there were significant differences between mid/low and high-proficiency subjects' mean scores ($p = .035$). ANOVA tests of proficiency by gender yielded significance for the subset of high-proficiency males across experiment groups, however, due to the small number of subjects in these groups (Top-down: $n = 2$; Bottom-up: $n = 4$; Control: $n = 2$), those results are not conclusive.

Treatment Group

Treatment as a variable accounted for variation among the data in two analyses: The top-down treatment group (females and males) performed significantly better than the other two experimental groups on inferred ideas ($p = .003$), and for the multiple-choice data, again, the top-down group outscored the other two ($p = .045$).

DISCUSSION

Some interesting results regarding gender were found in the present study. Looking at the effects of gender as a variable independent of treatment and proficiency shows that females performed significantly better than males on total recall, main ideas, and secondary ideas. In fact, females in every group outperformed males with only three exceptions: Males in the control group outperformed females in the control group on the multiple-choice test and on inferred ideas, and males in the top-down group outperformed all female (and male) groups on the multiple-choice test. However, the interaction of treatment was not significant on either assessment; that is, there were no significant differences between males' and females' mean re-call protocol and multiple-choice scores within each treatment group. On the other hand, there were significant differences in mean scores among male but not among female treatment groups, indicating that the males were less homogeneous as a group than were the females.

Why did females outperform males so consistently? Several studies reported on by Chavez (2001) suggest female superiority on achievement (e.g., Huebner, 1995; Wen & Johnson, 1997), final course grade (Nyikos, 1990; Sadker & Sadker, 1994), language proficiency (Boyle, 1987), and reading comprehension (Brantmeier, 2003a,b). Not all studies have shown that females outperform males, though. For example, Bacon (1992) found no significant differences between males and females in listening comprehension, and Feyten's (1991) study shows that "sex was not found to be a significant predictor of foreign language proficiency," though listening comprehension ability and prior exposure to the TL were (Chavez, 2001, p. 44). One possibility for the females' better performance on the recall but not on the multiple-choice test may be related to the assessment task and associated task goals. Previous research on learning styles has shown that females are considered to be more global learners, whereas males are more analytic (Oxford, 1993). As Bügel and Buunk (1996, p. 18) state: 'Summary tasks measure comprehension of the task as a whole.' It follows then, that females would perform better on a more global assessment such as the re-call protocol, and males on a discrete task such as the multiple-choice test.

Secondly, female students may possess a greater desire to please their teachers than do males (Chavez, 2001). Thus, the female subjects in the present study may have, whether consciously or not, tried to write more extensively on the essay format of the recall protocol than the male subjects did. Since the recall protocol was assessed on the basis of a number of story ideas included with no penalty for errors, the more the subject wrote, the better his or her chance for obtaining a higher score.

Returning to the research questions, the first question looks not only at gender but at the interaction of gender and treatment: Do males and females benefit similarly in different types of pre-reading strategy training, namely, in top-down and bottom-up strategies? The results suggest that male's and female's ability to make inferences improves after instruction in top-down strategies, as males and females in the top-down treatment groups performed significantly better than the other groups on inferred ideas. When comprehension is assessed by the multiple choice task, males seem to benefit more from the top-down treatment than do females. Males in the top-down treatment group outscored males in the other two groups to statistical significance, whereas the females' scores showed no significant difference.

What is interesting about the data with respect to the interaction of gender and treatment is the performance of males in the bottom-up versus the control groups. Males in the bottom-up group scored lower than males in the control group on all segments of the recall protocol and on the multiple-choice task.[7] In other words, male subjects who received pre-reading training in bottom-up strategies actually did worse than their cohorts who received no pre-reading training at all. This does not mean that bottom-up strategies should necessarily be excluded from pre-reading instruction. As previous research has shown, FL readers tend to rely more on bottom-up strategies when reading in the TL, and readers must know how and when to apply certain strategies. One might speculate that the male subjects in the bottom-up group focused too much on detail-oriented strategies to the detriment of their comprehension. Such behavior would further underscore the importance of strategy instruction that emphasizes appropriate use. The females in the bottom-up group, who may by nature rely more on global reading strategies than males, may have been better able to balance the detail-oriented strategy instruction with a more global reading style.

The role of proficiency in the efficacy of pre-reading training and in strategic benefits linked to gender seems limited based on the present study and depends on the data set. While high proficiency subjects in the top-down group outperformed high proficiency subjects in the other groups on inferred and main ideas, there were no significant differences on total recall and no significant differences among mid/low proficiency males and females, and any differences on the multiple-choice task cannot be linked statistically to proficiency. However, those results should be viewed cautiously due to the small number of subjects in each subset once participants were divided by proficiency and gender.

LIMITATIONS AND SUGGESTIONS
FOR FURTHER RESEARCH

Some limitations of the present study's research design bear mentioning. With regard to treatment, this study employed a single, short-term (i.e., cross-sectional) as opposed to a long-term (i.e., longitudinal) treatment. Perhaps with further training subjects would have benefitted more from the bottom-up strategies than was demonstrated in this study. Yet testing that hypothesis might prove detrimental to the reading ability of study participants who were to receive only the bottom-up treatment. Second, it is impossible to know whether subjects actually used the strategies in which they received pre-reading training. This, of course, is true of most research on strategy use. Third, due to the limited number of participants, it was not feasible to include a treatment group that incorporated both top-down and bottom-up strategy training. Further research should explore whether such a treatment would benefit participants more than would top-down treatment alone. Fourth, only one text-type was included in this study due to participants' time constraints. Though the choice and topic of text and text-type did not skew results since it had been identified as gender neutral through prior testing, further research might consider the role of text-type and topic in such a training study.

Limitations linked to assessment emerge from the difficulty of knowing whether the more global recall protocol task and the more analytical, discrete-point multiple-choice task affected the study outcomes. Since those two types of assessment reflect different learning styles and, by extension, strategy use, they measure comprehension in different ways, thus complicating interpretation of the results. Is either task biased toward one gender or certain types of learners? This inherent dilemma in assessment should be considered by researchers and FL instructors when testing reading comprehension.

CONCLUSIONS AND PEDAGOGICAL IMPLICATIONS

One primary objective of beginning- and intermediate-level language courses is to train students, longitudinally, in a sense, to read different types of texts at varying levels of difficulty, with the ultimate goal of preparing students to read challenging texts autonomously as they continue with their language study, whether they are canonical literary texts, advertising found in popular magazines, or Web sites. However, in the FL curriculum, relatively little attention is devoted to the explicit teaching of reading strategies. As a result, FL students are often unsure of how to read in the TL, possess little metacognitive awareness of strategies they use while reading in their NL, and do not know if those same strategies can be applied effectively to FL reading. FL instructors, on the other hand, are charged with the task of creating effective pre-, during-, and post-reading activities tailored to the needs of individuals, yet are time-efficient. Instructors are faced with many options for teaching reading strategies but are often unable to judge how effective particular strategies might be for learners whose learning styles may differ over a number of variables, gender being one.

Previous research suggests that males and females report using different strategies in FL reception. The results of the present study indicate that the top-down treatment benefitted both males and females on making inferences and on the multiple-choice test and benefitted all subjects considered to have high baseline proficiency. The bottom-up treatment did not benefit participants. In fact, it may have been disadvantageous, especially for males. The two types of assessment presented both a complicating and revealing element to the study, highlighting the need for FL instructors to keep task criteria and expectations in mind when creating pre-reading exercises and assessment measures.

Based on results of this study, the following recommendations for FL instructors can be made. First, keep in mind learner variables such as gender in the curricular planning and teaching of reading. Second, consider the types of assessment used to measure reading comprehension and whether they might be biased toward particular learning styles, and by extension, gender and strategy use. Third, expose learners to a variety of reading strategies in order to add to their current repertoire, reinforce the strategies they already use appropriately, and raise their awareness of appropriate strategy use. Fourth, when faced with time constraints for pre-reading strategy training, choose top-down pre-reading strategies as long as reading goals are consistent with more global, gist-oriented reading comprehension. Ultimately, it seems logical that all FL learners will benefit from regular exposure to diverse strategies, especially when their appropriate and effective use is emphasized. The results of this study, however, present empirical evidence that top-down strategic reading activities are more effective than and should be selected over bottom-up activities.

ACKNOWLEDGMENTS

The data and analyses presented in this article are drawn from my doctoral dissertation (Schueller, 1999). I am grateful to editors Cindy Brantmeier and JoAnn Hammadou Sullivan, as well as to two anonymous readers, for their feedback.

NOTES

1. In this chapter, foreign language (FL) refers to a language being learned or acquired outside of a target language environment, for example, German in the U.S.; second languages (L2) are those that are learned or acquired within a target language environment, for example, English in the United States. L2 is used here to indicate both foreign and second languages in general.
2. See, for example, Young (1993, p. 463–467) for a more comprehensive breakdown of top-down (i.e., global) and bottom-up (i.e., local) strategies.
3. The instrument used in many self-report studies is the Strategy Inventory for Language Learning (SILL), which was originally developed for the Army Research Institute and the Defense Language Institute. Several modified versions are in use today. The SILL is a 121-item, 5-point Likert scale instrument that asks subjects to report the frequency with which they use particular language learning strategies.
4. There was no attempt to organize group composition by proficiency, as this would have been too complicated.
5. Subjects were asked to role play one of the following situations (given to the subjects in German). **A.** Imagine you wake up hungry during the middle of the night. There wasn't much to eat for dinner and there isn't much food in the house. Your spouse is sleeping peacefully next to you. What would you do? **B.** You get up during the night to eat something even though you know that you are supposed to be rationing your food. How do you feel after you eat your midnight snack? Full? Guilty? Satisfied? What do you say to your spouse? Would you lie?
6. In the following example of this activity, the correct answer would be "library" because a library is semantically related to book: **BOOK:** (1) post office, (2) library, (3) grocery store, (4) restaurant. This activity was modeled after the "Wortfelder" (word field) exercises in the beginning German textbook *Vorsprung* (Lovik et al., 1997).
7. Females in the bottom-up group outperformed females in the control on all tasks except for secondary ideas.

REFERENCES

Bacon, S. M. (1992). The relationship between gender, comprehension, processing strategies, and cognitive and affective response in foreign language listening. *Modern Language Journal, 76,* 160–176.

Bacon, S. M., & Finnemann, M. D. (1992). Sex differences in self-reported beliefs about foreign language learning and authentic oral and written input. *Language Learning, 42,* 471–495.

Barnett, M. A. (1988). Reading through context: How real and perceived strategy use affects L2 comprehension. *Modern Language Journal, 72,* 150–162.

Bernhardt, E. B. (1983). Syntactic and lexical/semantic skill in foreign language reading comprehension: The Immediate Recall Protocol. *Die Unterrichtspraxis, 16,* 27–33.

Block, E. (1986). The comprehension strategies of second language readers. *TESOL Quarterly, 20,* 463–484.

Boyle, J. P. (1987). Sex differences in listening vocabulary. *Language Learning, 37,* 273–284.

Brantmeier, C. (2001). Second language reading research on passage content and gender: Challenges for the intermediate level curriculum. *Foreign Language Annals, 34,* 325–333.

Brantmeier, C. (2003a). Does gender make a difference? Passage content and comprehension in second language reading. *Reading in a Foreign Language, 15,* 1–24.

Brantmeir, C. (2003b). Beyond linguistic knowledge: Individual differences in second language reading. *Foreign Language Annals, 36,* 33–43.

Bügel, K., & Buunk, R. P. (1996). Sex differences in foreign language text comprehension: The role of interests and prior knowledge. *Modern Language Journal, 80,* 15–31.

Carrell, P. L. (1989). Metacognitive awareness and second language reading. *Modern Language Journal, 73,* 121–133.

Carrell, P. L. (1991). Second language reading: Reading ability or language proficiency? *Applied Linguistics, 12,* 159–179.

Chavez, M. (2001). *Gender in the language classroom.* Boston: McGraw-Hill.

Ehrman, M. E., & Oxford, R. L. (1989). Effects of sex differences, career choice, and psychological type on adults' language learning strategies. *Modern Language Journal, 73,* 1–13.

Feyten, C. M. (1991). The power of listening ability: An overlooked dimension in language acquisition. *Modern Language Journal, 75,* 173–180.

Green, J. M., & Oxford, R. L. (1995). A closer look at learning strategies, L2 proficiency, and gender. *TESOL Quarterly, 29,* 261–297.

Horiba, Y. (1996). Comprehension processes in L2 reading: Language competence, textual coherence, and inferences. *Studies in Second Language Acquisition, 18,* 433–473.

Huebner, T. (1995). A framework for investigating the effectiveness of study abroad programs. In C. Kramsch (Ed.), *Redefining the boundaries of language study* (pp. 185–217). AAUSC Annual Volumes. Boston: Heinle & Heinle.

Kern, R. G. (1989). Second language reading strategy instruction: Its effects on comprehension and word inference ability. *Modern Language Journal, 73*, 135–149.

Kim, S.-A. (1995). Types and sources of problems in L2 reading: A qualitative analysis of the recall protocols by Korean high school students. *Foreign Language Annals, 28*, 49–70.

Lee, J. F. (1986). On the use of the recall task to measure L2 reading comprehension. *Studies in Second Language Acquisition, 8*, 201–212.

Lovik, T. A., Guy, J. D., & Chavez, M. (1997). *Vorsprung: An introduction to the German language and culture for communication*. Boston: Houghton Mifflin.

MacIntyre, P. D., & Noels, K. A. (1996). Using social- psychological variables to predict the use of language learning strategies. *Foreign Language Annals, 29*, 373–386.

Nyikos, M. (1990). Sex-related differences in adult language learning: Socialization and memory factors. *Modern Language Journal, 74*, 273–287.

Oxford, R. L. (1993). Gender differences in styles and strategies for language learning: What do they mean? Should we pay attention? In J. E. Alatis (Ed.), *Strategic interaction and language acquisition: Theory, practice and research* (pp. 541–558). Georgetown University Roundtable on Languages and Linguistics. Washington DC: Georgetown University Press.

Oxford, R. L., & Nyikos, M. (1989). Variables affecting choice of language learning strategies by university students. *Modern Language Journal, 73*, 291–300.

Sadker, M., & Sadker, D. (1994). *Failing at fairness: How America's schools cheat girls*. New York: Charles Schribner's Sons.

Schmeck, R. (1983). Learning styles of college students. In R. F. Dillon & R. R. Schmeck (Eds.), *Individual differences in cognition* (pp. 223–279). New York: Academic Press.

Schueller, J. (1999). *The effects of two types of strategic training on foreign language reading comprehension: An analysis by gender and proficiency*. University of Wisconsin-Madison dissertation.

Schultz, R. (1983). From word to meaning: Foreign language reading instruction after the elementary course. *Modern Language Journal, 67*, 127–134.

Taglieber, L. K., Johnson, L. L., & Yarbrough, D. B. (1988). Effects of prereading activities on EFL reading by Brazilian college students. *TESOL Quarterly, 22*, 455–472.

Wen, Q.-F., & Johnson, R. K. (1997). L2 learner variables and English achievement: A study of tertiary-level English majors in China. *Applied Linguistics, 18*, 27–48.

Young, D. (1993). Processing strategies of foreign language readers: Authentic and edited input. *Foreign Language Annals, 26*, 451–468.

Young, D., & Oxford, R. L. (1997). A gender-related analysis of strategies used to process written input in the native language and a foreign language. *Applied Language Learning, 8*, 43–73.

APPENDIX
Multiple-Choice Questions to *Das Brot*

1. Warum wachte die Frau auf?
    a. Es war zu still.
    b. Sie hörte ihren Mann nicht atmen.
    c. Sie hatte etwas gehört.
    d. Weil es halb drei war.
2. Was machte ihr Mann in der Küche?
    a. Er machte das Tischtuch sauber.
    b. Er machte die Fliesen sauber.
    c. Er nahm Brot.
    d. Er holte Brot für seine Frau.
3. Warum ging der Mann in die Küche?
    a. Weil es windig war and die Dachrinne klapperte.
    b. Er hatte vergessen, das Licht auszumachen.
    c. Er wollte die Krümel von dem Tischtuch abwischen.
    d. Er hatte Hunger.
4. Warum log der Mann?
    a. Weil er die Küche schmutzig gemacht hatte.
    b. Weil er sich wahrscheinlich schuldig
    c. Weil seine Frau sehr alt aussah.
    d. Weil sie schon neununddreißig Jahre verheiratet waren.
5. Warum gab die Frau ihm am nächsten Abend vier Scheiben Brot?
    a. Die Frau wußte, daß er Hunger hatte.
    b. Die Frau hatte keinen Hunger.
    c. Der Mann hat die Frau um vier Scheiben gebeten.
    d. Das Brot schmeckte der Frau nicht.

CPSIA information can be obtained at www.ICGtesting.com
Printed in the USA
LVOW071717260413

331089LV00001B/9/P